WOK
COOKING

WOK COOKING

DISCOVER THE QUICK AND SIMPLE SECRETS OF WOK COOKING

BRIDGET JONES

CHARTWELL
BOOKS, INC.

A QUINTET BOOK

Published by Chartwell Books
A Division of Book Sales, Inc.
PO Box 7100, Edison,
New Jersey 08818-7100

This edition produced for sale in the U.S.A.,
its territories and dependencies only.

ISBN 0-7858-0278-9

Reprinted 1995

This book was designed and produced by
Quintet Publishing Limited
6 Blundell Street
London N7 9BH

Creative Director: Richard Dewing
Designers: Stuart Walden, Ian Hunt
Project Editor: William Hemsley
Illustrator: Syrah Arnold
Photographer: Trevor Wood

Typeset in Great Britain by
Central Southern Typesetters, Eastbourne
Manufactured by J Film Process Singapore Pte Ltd.
Printed in Singapore by Star Standard Industries Pte Ltd.

CONTENTS

FOREWORD

Stir frying is often classified, quite correctly, as a cooking method for oriental dishes or for "healthy" meals since it is authentic to the first category and thoroughly appropriate to the second. However, in the pages that follow, I would like to demonstrate that the technique of stir frying can be as exotic or homely, as healthy or rich, and as simple or as complicated, as you wish to make it.

The oriental origins have produced a distinct style of food preparation and mixing which has dominated stir fry cooking but, given that a few basic rules are followed, a range of multi-national dishes may be created. For beginners, there are notes on the choice of cooking equipment, from the ideal options through to improvising, and a few comments which may be helpful if you are thinking of buying a new stir fry pan. The rest of the introduction sets out simple guidelines for the choice of ingredients, the techniques for cutting and flavoring them, and the importance of cooking different foods in the right order to achieve perfect results.

Hopefully, once you have read the opening pages you will appreciate the principles of this quick cooking method, so that you may look upon the recipes as a basis for extending your existing culinary repertoire and experimenting with new ideas or interesting seasonings.

Take advantage of the cornucopia of ingredients now available from all corners of the world – the exotic vegetables and fruit; fragrant spices and preserves; contrasting grains and cereals; and quick-to-cook seafood, poultry or meat. Look upon your stir fry pan as an essential item for practical or the latest cooking – whether to boost the healthy side of a balanced everyday diet or to conjure up fashionable meals in minutes – and it will soon become one of the best-used items in the kitchen. Here's to quick cooking and good eating – bon appetite!

Utensils – Essential Equipment for Preparation and Cooking

The key piece of equipment is, of course, the cooking pan and the most important feature is size: a good stir fry skillet or pan must hold a large volume of ingredients, at the same time allowing sufficient room for stirring and turning them during cooking. The recipes do not give specific information on the type of pan because it is unnecessary; if you are new to stir frying, read the following notes before attempting the recipes.

Woks

A wok is the most suitable pan for the majority of stir frying but there is a choice of types, from traditional cook pans to electric appliances.

CARBON STEEL WOK The traditional wok is made from thin, uncoated carbon steel. It is deeply curved with a stout wooden handle, which is designed for lifting, tilting and shaking the pan using one hand, leaving the other hand free for using a scoop to stir the ingredients. The domed pan fits over a flaming brazier in Chinese restaurants, but at home a rack may be used to stabilize a wok on an electric stove top, or if necessary, over a gas burner. However, depending on how the pan stands on a gas stove top, the rack may be redundant.

This traditional type of wok conducts heat well, provides a large surface area for cooking and it is highly responsive to changes in heat. However, a carbon steel wok must be used regularly and kept oiled to prevent rusting between use. A new wok should be washed in hot soapy water to remove any protective coating, then tempered or seasoned. This involves heating a small amount of oil in the wok, rubbing it over all the surface of the pan, until smoking hot but not burning. The pan should be wiped out with absorbent paper towels. The outside and any exposed metal around the edge of the handle must be oiled. Wipe with clean absorbent paper towels before storage or use. After each use, the pan must be wiped out and oiled before storage.

Two designs of wok, one with the traditional long wooden handle and the other with two carrying handles. The brush may be used to oil woks, and the strainers are useful accessories for some recipes.

Depending upon the food cooked, there are two ways of cleaning the wok. Ideally, wipe out the pan with paper towels, then sprinkle in some salt and pour in a little oil. Heat this and remove the pan from the heat. Use a pad of absorbent kitchen paper to clean the wok – the salt acts as a scouring agent and removes food residue. Wipe out all the oil and salt, then heat the wok again with a little fresh oil before wiping it clean. If the food has left a cooked-on coating of sauce, the pan must be washed, dried and tempered. This method of scouring with oil and salt is best for the majority of oil-based stir frying.

I find the most practical way of storing a carbon steel wok is to keep it well greased in a large bag with an elastic band around the handle. I reserve my carbon steel wok for oriental and vegetable stir fries, and for dishes with small amounts of meat and grains. The carbon steel pan is not suitable for stir frying fruit.

STAINLESS STEEL AND NON-STICK WOKS These are far easier to look after than a carbon steel pan. They may be washed in hot soapy water, dried and stored according to the manufacturer's instructions.

The quality of the pans varies enormously. In general they are all slightly less responsive to changes in heat than carbon steel. Unlike carbon steel woks, the cheapest of which (purchased in an oriental supermarket) is often the best, price is often a good indication of quality within this group.

Consider the shape of the pan – many are smaller than expected of an authentic wok and they may have very flat bases, putting them on a par with a skillet rather than a wok. A pan with a small, quite flat base may not be the best buy and a large conventional frying pan with deep sides may provide more surface area for cooking. Before buying, check the using instructions that go with the pan because some non-stick finishes are not suitable for cooking over high heat, therefore they are not ideal for the majority of stir frying. Inexpensive non-stick finishes can deteriorate rapidly when used over high heat and when the food is stirred constantly (even using the correct non-stick coated utensils).

ELECTRIC WOKS I have little experience of these but was surprised with the quality of the results when I tested one model. I found the pan to be more responsive than I had expected and suitable for cooking large quantities. This may not be the purist's option but a work-top appliance is useful in many kitchens. Remember to follow carefully the manufacturer's instructions for use and cleaning.

Frying pans and skillets

A wok is not essential for stir frying; a frying pan or skillet used for this purpose should be large, with deep sides. Ideally, opt for a pan with slightly sloping sides and a curved edge around the base – this allows the food to be turned easily. The term skillet is a slightly confusing one – it is used sometimes as a generic American term for a frying pan, or it may refer to a pan which is about 5 cm/2 in deep (or slightly larger), suitable for frying, with a lid. A large skillet is ideal for stir frying as the depth of the sides prevents food from spilling during stirring and cooking.

A sauté pan is usually large with deep sides and, since sautéing is similar to stir frying in that the food is cooked over high heat and stirred during cooking (although less vigorously), this type of pan is suitable for stir frying.

Heavy, non-stick coated cast iron pans may be used for stir frying, but usually they have to be heated slowly and kept over a medium rather than high heat. The manufacturer may state that the pan should not be heated empty, therefore a coating of oil or fat should be added. The pan may be used for stir frying once hot, but the heat is not as fierce and the pan is not as responsive, taking a long time to cool or react to changes in temperature. These pans are suitable for stir frying fruit or other ingredients that are not necessarily cooked over fierce heat.

FEATURES TO LOOK FOR IN A PAN

▮ Materials and finishes that withstand high heat.

▮ A large cooking surface and/or room for pushing cooked ingredients to one side (for example the sides of a wok).

▮ A pan with deep sides to prevent food spillages during stirring.

▮ A long, sturdy handle which is a poor conductor of heat so that it stays cool during cooking.

▮ A pan with a lid can be useful if you intend using stir frying as one part of a longer cooking process – avoid a carbon steel lid for a wok as it rusts easily; look for a domed steel lid.

MAKING DO – WHAT TO AVOID

Even though a wok may be the ideal, improvising is part of the fun and skill of cooking. If you literally own just one saucepan, given that it is designed for putting over high heat and it has a surface area large enough for the quantities of food, then go ahead and stir fry in it!

● Preparation and cooking utensils

The preparation of food is equally as important as the cooking technique, involving a good deal of cutting up.

CHOPPING BOARDS Have a very large chopping board that can be scrubbed in hot soapy water. For the sake of food safety and hygiene, remember that wood is absorbent and easily damaged, allowing food particles to be trapped and bacteria to grow. If you do have a wooden board, scrub it in very hot water, using a mild solution of bleach or an abrasive cleaner. Rinse and thoroughly dry it AFTER EVERY USE.

Plastic-based boards are non-absorbent, therefore less likely to be a food safety risk. However, these too must be scrubbed after each use to clean them.

An important point to remember is that the board must be sufficiently spacious to cut a large volume of ingredients. There is nothing more frustrating than trying to cut even-sized slivers when there is barely room to fit the point of a knife between ingredients on the surface of the board!

KNIVES A good knife is essential – select a medium or large cook's knife with a strong blade which sharpens to an acute cutting edge. Never buy a knife by looks and technical information alone – pick it up and feel it, hold it as though to cut and try to get a feeling for how it manoeuvres. Assess several different types of knives before buying, looking for one which feels well balanced and comfortable. Wooden handles may look attractive but they require care and attention if they are to last, and they are definitely not dishwasher proof – in fact they should never be left in water, except for a brief (but thorough) wash. Wood also needs oiling occasionally. If this is unlikely to suit your kitchen habits, a good-quality dishwasher-proof knife may be the better option. Whichever you decide upon, look for a knife with a handle riveted to the blade.

To go with your knife, you need a good quality steel to sharpen it – look for one with a guard to protect your hand should the knife slip up to the handle. Some oriental supermarkets and hardware shops sell sharpening stones – look for one that has both coarse and fine sides.

There are different ways of using a steel: slide the knife blade along the surface, working away from you.

Start with the wide end of the blade above and at the top of the steel, then slide it down until the point of the knife is at the tip of the steel. Repeat with the knife underneath the steel to work on the upper edge of the knife's blade.

Alternatively, have the knife point at the top of the steel, then work down the steel until the top of the blade is at its tip. Repeat with the knife underneath the steel.

If you are very inexperienced with handling knives, or prone to accidents, then hold the steel vertical, with its point on a firm board or surface. Work the knife down its length – this avoids any danger of the knife slipping towards your wrist.

Whichever method you use, repeat the process several times until the knife blade is sharp, then wash and dry it before use. Sharpen knives frequently, in theory before each use and during use when cutting quantities of ingredients.

STIRRING UTENSILS A large scoop or flat metal spatula, both with strong handles, are the perfect partners for a carbon steel wok. If you are using a non-stick pan, you will need a suitable plastic or non-stick coated spatula or slice. A slotted spoon (or draining spoon) may be used instead.

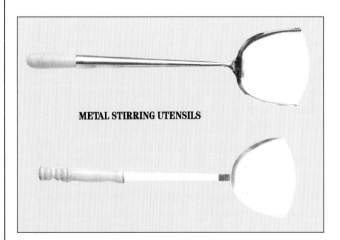

METAL STIRRING UTENSILS

ESSENTIAL ACCESSORIES Ingredients have to be prepared before you begin to stir fry them, so a selection of bowls or basins is useful for holding the ingredients. Cereal bowls or plastic containers may be used – the size and number depend on the dish being prepared.

Food at its Best – Selecting Ingredients

Quick cooking brings out the flavor of food to the full, but the right choice of ingredients is vital.

Fish and seafood

The majority of fish and seafood cooks quickly, so from the timing angle they are suitable for stir frying. However, thin fish fillets that break up easily during cooking are not suitable. Thicker portions of firm white fish, shrimp, scallops, mussels, oysters and squid are all examples of seafood for stir frying.

Look for fresh fish which is moist, bright and firm. Avoid any that smells strong or looks dull and old. Buy from a reputable source and remember that the fish seller will do a lot of the preparation for you.

Poultry

All types of poultry are suitable for stir frying because they cook quickly to give tender results. Prime cuts of breast fillet are best.

Meat

Tender cuts of meat recommended for broiling or frying are suitable for stir frying. Tougher pieces that require lengthy stewing or braising should be avoided. All pork is tender, but some cuts require more trimming to remove fat and gristle or sinews than others. Similarly, most cuts of lamb are suitable for stir frying, the prime choice being loin, fillet or leg meat.

Trim the excess fat and all gristle before cutting meat into thin pieces across the grain. Meat may be half frozen for easy slicing into paper-thin pieces.

Vegetables

The majority of vegetables may be stir fried for different lengths of time, according to how quickly they cook. For example, root vegetables, such as potatoes, require longer cooking than bean sprouts or Chinese leaves. The way in which the vegetables are cut also contributes to the cooking time.

Select very fresh vegetables in prime condition because second-rate ingredients are unsuitable for stir frying. Look for firm, unbruised vegetables with crisp leaves and a good color. Avoid bruised or damaged specimens, root vegetables that are soft or wrinkled, and cabbages or other greens that are faded, yellowing or limp. Peppers, tomatoes and eggplants should be firm and bright.

Cereals, pulses and grains

Cooked cereals, beans and grains may be stir fried to make satisfying meals. It is important to avoid overcooking them before stir frying as they may break up or become very soft.

If these ingredients are cooked and cooled before stir frying, always ensure they are thoroughly reheated before serving to destroy any bacteria, which may have multiplied on cooling and during re-warming.

Fruit

Firm fruits respond well to stir frying and the softer types may be added during the final stages of cooking. Select perfect fresh fruit and prepare it just before cooking unless it is left to macerate as part of the recipe.

Dried and canned fruit are also suitable for stir frying – the types of dried fruit which are ready to eat are particularly useful.

Oils and fats

The choice of fat is important, not only for flavor but also for the results in cooking. Fats melt at different temperatures, for example, oil, lard, butter, and margarine are all liquid at different temperatures.

When fats are heated chemical changes take place at varying temperatures, causing the fat to change in appearance and, eventually, flavor. If you have never noticed the way in which oils react to heating, then heat a few samples and watch. Butter tends to brown and burn at a lower temperature than some oils even though its melting temperature is higher.

Clarified butter is more suitable for frying as it does not break down as easily. It is prepared by melting the butter, then simmering it gently until a sediment forms and sizzling ceases. At this stage the solids are precipitated and the water content has evaporated (the sizzling continues until the water is driven off). The butter should be strained through cheesecloth, the solids discarded, and the liquid cooled before storage.

Margarines do not reach as high a cooking temperature and are not ideal for stir frying. Low fat spreads are not suitable for frying.

Olive oil smokes at a comparatively low temperature. It is useful for stir frying many ingredients or in dishes to which it contributes flavor.

Peanut oil may be heated to a higher temperature before it begins to smoke. Therefore, it is ideal for cooking ingredients that benefit from rapid cooking and having a crisp outer surface.

Sunflower, corn and vegetable oils are all suitable, and they all reach temperatures high enough to make food brown and crisp. More importantly, they do not smoke and 'burn' too easily, and are therefore useful for prolonged frying at a high temperature.

Sesame oil and nut oils (walnut and hazelnut) are used for their flavor, but they overheat easily. Since they have distinct flavors, they are best used in small quantities as flavorings rather than the main cooking mediums. For example, a little of any one of these oils may be added to the mixture for meatballs or used in marinades, or a little sesame oil may be combined with sunflower or peanut oil for cooking.

All-important Techniques

Stir frying is an easy, relaxed cooking method, which should not be dominated by pedantic do's and don'ts; however, the secret of success lies in efficient advance prerparation of all ingredients. A few attempts at this cooking method is enough to make each cook their own expert.

Washing, draining and drying

Make sure all vegetables are clean before cutting and cooking. Some types are easier to wash after cutting, for example leeks. Drain most vegetables in a colander, small pieces in a strainer, and mop them on absorbent paper towels before cooking to prevent spitting.

Preparation and cutting

Stir frying is speedy, so all ingredients should be cut to cook quickly and evenly. The size of the pieces depends on the texture and cooking requirements of the food as much as on the expected result and appearance of the dish. Here is a list of some of the techniques used in the recipes.

SLICES Thick or thin, depending on how much cooking is required and the finished texture. Make sure slices are even.

Sliced

DIAGONAL SLICES Cut into slices at an angle. For example, green onions and celery sticks should have the end cut off at an angle, then all the slices should be cut at an angle to give evenly thick, slanting slices.

FINGERS OR STICKS Cut fairly thick slices, then cut these into fingers or sticks. Cucumber and zucchini should be cut into lengths, then quartered lengthwise.

THIN STICKS Finer than fingers but not as delicate as matchstick strips, these are about ¼ in thick.

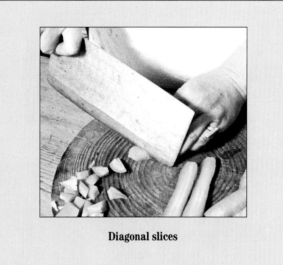

Diagonal slices

MATCHSTICK STRIPS Literally the size of matchsticks, these should be fine and even. They cook very quickly: useful for garnish – small piles of ingredients may be arranged Japanese style.

SHREDDED Cut into thin slices, then across into fine pieces. Firm cabbage and similar leaves may be shredded by cutting into chunks, then thinly slicing.

GRATED Use the coarse blade on a grater and discard the last, small chunk which cannot be processed.

CHOPPED Cut slices, thin sticks, then cut across to chop the ingredient. Halve and slice an onion, then cut across the slices so that they fall into small, reasonably even, pieces, though not as even as those produced by dicing. The pieces should be small unless roughly chopped, in which case they can be slightly larger and less even. Chop herbs by using a large sharp knife and a guillotine action.

DICED Cut into small, even cubes – about ¼ in or slightly larger.

Shredded

In cubing and dicing, the food is first cut into slices and then in the opposite direction.

CUBED Cut larger cubes than required for dice – between ½ in and 1 in – but even in size.

CHUNKS Slightly larger than cubed and less even. No need to trim food into a neat square shape.

Marinating and macerating

These are both terms relating to soaking food before cooking or eating. Marinating is used for savory foods and macerating is the term for soaking fruit before use in cooking or before eating.

There are two main reasons for soaking food – to impart flavor to it and to tenderize tough ingredients. Marinating meat in selected ingredients improves the texture as well as the flavor. Herbs, spices, fruit, wine and acids are all common ingredients for marinades. The ingredients may be mixed and used raw, or liquids may be heated with flavorings, cooled and used as a marinade. The food may be soaked for anything from 30 minutes to three days, depending on the food and the required results.

When marinating for long periods, the food should be absolutely fresh – particularly meat and poultry. The food should always be covered and kept in a cool place; if left for longer than a couple of hours it must be placed in the refrigerator, particularly in warm weather. Turn and rearrange food during marinating to keep the ingredients evenly coated in the flavorings.

Stir frying techniques

Have all the ingredients prepared and ready for adding to the pan. Make sure that the diners are ready to eat too, as many stir fry dishes do not keep well once they have been cooked.

Heat the fat and add the ingredients that require longest cooking first. When they are part cooked, add the next batch of ingredients. Continue adding the ingredients in stages so that they are all cooked together when the dish is complete. In some cases, the additional ingredients may be mixed directly with the food in the pan, in others the part-cooked food should be pushed to one side and the new items stir fried quickly before all the food is combined.

TIMING STIR FRYING Giving exact timings for stir frying is difficult and can be misleading. The time necessary to cook food depends not only on the way it is cut and the heat of the pan, but on the volume of other ingredients, and the size of the cooking pan also plays a role. If the pan is full, the new ingredients take longer to cook; if a large, spacious pan is used the food has better contact with the base and it cooks more quickly.

With some commonsense and a bit of experience, you will soon recognize the right moment to add the next batch of ingredients. Take particular care to insure that poultry is well cooked by checking the pieces at each cooking stage and before serving. If there are any signs of blood in the juices, the poultry is not cooked sufficiently.

STIR BRAISING This is similar to stir frying but with moisture in the pan, and it is often the natural follow-on technique after stir frying. Once the ingredients are stir fried, stock or other liquids are added and the cooking continues, with the ingredients being stirred, until the dish is complete and any sauce is reduced or thickened.

SERVING Lastly, remember that foods that are cooked quickly benefit from immediate serving, so transfer the food to a heated serving dish or indiviudal plates promptly. Have garnishes or accompaniments ready so that the complete course may be served at once. Remember that the wok or pan may be taken to the table and kept warm over a burner.

STIR FRYING FOR APPETIZERS

A stir fried first course can be light, colorful and thoroughly appetizing; perfect, in fact, for getting a meal off to a good beginning. Have all the ingredients organized, the pan on the stove top (but not heated), and you can spring into action while guests relax over pre-dinner drinks.

If the cooking time is especially short, remember to insure everyone is sitting down – or at least making for the table – before you stir fry: better to have them waiting for a few minutes than to allow a splendid dish to cool and maybe spoil.

As well as the ideas in this chapter, many main-course stir fried dishes are easily adapted to serving as appetizers by reducing the quantities of ingredients. Similarly, you can double up the amounts in these recipes to make a selection of delicious light lunches or suppers.

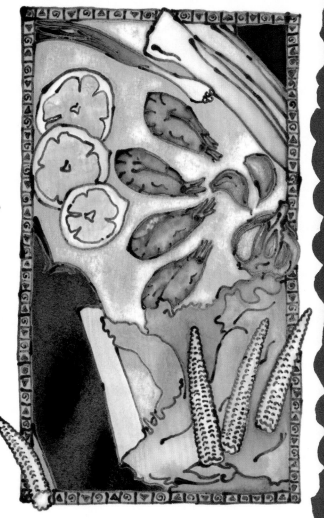

● Spicy Oriental Squid

When the pieces of squid are stir fried they curl to expose the diamond cuts. The choice of cooking oil is important to achieve a high temperature and satisfactorily crisp results.

SERVES 4

12 squid, cleaned (see page 000)	2 garlic cloves, crushed
juice of 1 lemon	2 tsp sesame oil
1 green chili, seeded and chopped	⅓ cup peanut oil
	1 red bell pepper, diced
¼ tsp five spice powder	4 green onions, thinly sliced
	⅓ cup soy sauce

The tentacles may be used or not as preferred. Slit the squid body sacs lengthwise, then cut each into 2 – 3 pieces. Using a small, sharp pointed knife, score a zig-zag pattern on the inside of the pieces of squid. Do not cut right through the squid – simply mark a trellis pattern in the flesh.

Place the squid pieces in a basin. Add the lemon juice, chili, five spice powder, garlic and sesame oil, and mix well to coat all the pieces in seasoning. Cover and leave to marinate for at least an hour – if possible leave the squid for 3 – 4 hours.

Heat the peanut oil until shimmering, then stir fry the squid until browned. The pieces should curl to expose the attractive diamond cuts. Use a slotted spoon to remove the pieces from the pan and divide them between serving plates.

Pour off any excess oil from the pan, if necessary, leaving just enough to cook the vegetables. Stir fry the pepper and green onions for 1 – 2 minutes, then sprinkle in the soy sauce and stir for a few seconds. Spoon the vegetable mixture and juices over the squid and serve at once.

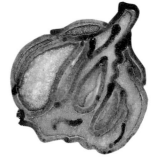

Golden Baby Corn with Shrimps

SERVES 4

1 garlic clove, crushed
¼ tsp turmeric
3 tbsp light soy sauce
3 tbsp medium sherry
½ lb whole baby corn cobs
¼ cup oil

1 celery stalk, cut in short, fine
    strips
4 green onions, shredded
¼ Iceberg lettuce, coarsely
    shredded
½ lb peeled and cooked
    shrimps or prawns
2 tsp grated lemon zest

Mix the garlic, turmeric, soy sauce and sherry in a large basin. Add the corn cobs and toss well to coat them in the seasonings. Cover and set aside for at least 30 minutes. The corn may be left to marinate for as long as several hours.

Heat 3 tablespoons of the oil and stir fry the celery for 30 seconds. Use a draining spoon to add the corn, reserving the juices. Stir fry the corn for 4 – 5 minutes. Mix in the green onions and cook for 1 minute before stirring in the lettuce. Add the juices from the corn and stir fry for a further 30 – 60 seconds. The lettuce should still be crisp.

Divide the mixture between four warmed plates or dishes. Add the remaining oil to the pan. Stir fry the shrimps and lemon zest for 30 seconds, or until hot, then divide between the portions of corn. Serve at once.

COOK'S TIP

If using frozen shrimps or prawns in this, or any other recipe, remember to weigh them after thawing and draining.

Scallops with Avocado

This is a good way of stretching a few large scallops to serve four. Serve thin bread and butter or melba toast with this starter.

SERVES 4

1 lime
1 bunch watercress
2 avocados

large knob of butter
a little oil
8 large scallops, sliced
salt and white pepper

Cut a thin strip of rind from around the middle of the lime, then slice this across into very fine shreds. Quarter the lime and set it aside. Trim the stalks off the watercress.

Halve the avocado, discard the pit and cut the flesh into quarters. Remove the peel, then slice the avocado quarters and arrange the slices on serving plates.

Heat the butter with a little oil. Add the lime rind and cook for a few seconds. Add the scallops with the watercress and stir fry for 1 – 2 minutes, or until the scallops are just cooked. They are ready when just firm – overcook them and they become tough. Divide the scallops between the plates and add a wedge of lime to each portion. Serve at once – the lime juice may be squeezed over the scallops before they are eaten.

GOLDEN BABY CORN

● Vegetable Snow Pancakes

Light pancakes made from egg whites and flavored with green onions are the ideal base on which to serve mixed vegetables. Large white radish or mooli, daikon in Japanese cuisine, peps up the already delicious broccoli and mushroom mixture.

SERVES 4
2 egg whites	½ lb broccoli
2 tbsp cornstarch	½ lb mushrooms, thinly
salt	sliced
2 green onions, finely chopped	3 tbsp soy sauce
	1 tbsp superfine sugar
STIR FRIED VEGETABLES	1 tbsp rice vinegar or cider
2 in piece white radish,	vinegar
peeled	oil for cooking
	3 tbsp sesame seeds

Lightly whisk the egg whites with 3 tablespoons water, adding the cornstarch a teaspoonful at a time. Whisk in a little salt, then stir in the green onions.

Cut the white radish lengthwise into thin slices, then cut the slices into fine strips. Place these in a bowl. Cut the broccoli into small pieces and mix them with the radish. Place the mushroom slices in a separate bowl and add the soy sauce, sugar and vinegar. Mix well but try not to break up the mushroom slices. Cover and set the mixture aside.

The pancakes may be cooked individually in a wok or three to four at a time in a large skillet. Heat a little oil, then lightly whisk the egg-white batter and pour a spoonful into the pan to make a thin round pancake. Cook until set and browned underneath, then turn and cook the second side until lightly browned. Drain the pancakes on absorbent paper towels and keep them hot. Make eight small pancakes.

Heat a little oil, then use a draining spoon to add the mushrooms. Stir fry over high heat for about 1 minute, until the mushrooms are browned. Add the radish and broccoli and continue cooking for about 3 minutes. Stir in the sesame seeds and cook for 1 minute, then pour in the juices from marinating the mushrooms.

Arrange the pancakes on individual plates, then top each with a portion of the stir-fried vegetables. Serve the dish at once.

Eggplant Toppers

This is an interesting and unusual opening for a
Mediterranean-style meal.

SERVES 4

1 large eggplant	1 small onion, halved and thinly sliced
salt and freshly ground black pepper	2 small white turnips, cut in fine strips
4 tomatoes, peeled and seeded	4 slices cooked ham, cut in fine strips
½ cup olive oil	4 basil sprigs, shredded
1 garlic clove, crushed	

Trim the eggplant and cut off a thin slice of peel,
lengthwise, from both sides. Cut the rest of the eggplant
into four long slices. Place these in a colander and
sprinkle with salt. Leave over a bowl for 20 minutes,
then rinse and pat dry on absorbent paper towels. Cut
the tomatoes into strips.

Heat ⅓ cup of the oil and add the eggplant slices.
Turn them after a few seconds, then cook until lightly
browned. Turn the slices again to brown the second
side. Transfer to serving plates and keep hot.

Heat the remaining oil. Add the garlic, onion and
turnips, then stir fry the mixture for about 5 minutes,
until the vegetables are cooked but still crunchy. Stir in
the tomatoes, ham and seasoning, and cook the mixture
for about 30 seconds.

Spoon the vegetable mixture over the eggplant slices
and top each portion with shredded basil. Serve at once
with some crusty bread to mop up the juices.

PEELING AND SEEDING TOMATOES

There are two ways of peeling tomatoes. The first is
useful for firm fruit: spear a tomato on a metal fork,
then hold it oiver a gas flame, turning the fork, until
the skin blisters and bursts. Rub off the skin under
cold water. When peeling a large quantity of tomatoes, place in a bowl and pour freshly boiling water
over them. Leave the fruit for 30 – 60 seconds, the
shorter time for very ripe tomatoes. Drain the
tomatoes and slit their skins with the point of a
knife – the skin should peel off easily.

To remove the seeds, halve a tomato, then use a
small teaspoon to scoop out the seeds, leaving the
shell and central part intact.

PEPPERAMA

Pepperama

This is a terrific summer starter – ideal for barbecues as you can heat the wok over the charcoal. It also makes a tempting side dish for kebabs or plain broiled meats.

SERVES 4

⅓ cup raisins

3 tbsp red wine

20 black olives, pitted and sliced

⅓ cup chopped fresh parsley

2 tsp grated lemon zest

4 large bell peppers, preferably red, green, yellow and orange

3 tbsp olive oil

¼ cup pine nuts

salt and freshly ground black pepper

Heat the raisins and wine in a small saucepan until boiling, then set aside. Alternatively, place them in a small basin or suitable mug and cook in the microwave on full power for about 30 seconds, until hot. Mix the olives, parsley and lemon zest.

Halve the peppers lengthwise, remove the core and all seeds, then slice the shells into thin strips. Heat the oil and stir fry the pine nuts for a minute or so, until they are just beginning to change color. Add the pepper strips and continue to stir fry for 4 – 5 minutes. Stir in the raisins with their juices and add seasoning to taste. Cook for a few seconds, then spread out the peppers on individual plates or one large platter. Top with the olive mixture and serve.

Vegetable Cups with Tapenade

These stir-fried vegetables in lettuce leaves are topped with tapenade to taste, then rolled up and eaten. The tapenade is highly seasoned to flavor the unsalted, stir-fried vegetables. Do not overfill the lettuce leaves, and remember to provide large napkins or finger bowls for cleaning oily fingers.

SERVES 4

TAPENADE

6 oz black olives, stoned

2 oz can anchovy fillets

3 tbsp capers

1 large garlic clove, crushed

freshly ground black pepper

3 tbsp lemon juice

about ¼ cup olive oil

STIR FRY VEGETABLES

1 fennel bulb

4 celery stalks

3 tbsp olive oil

½ small onion, thinly sliced (a red onion gives the best flavor)

15 oz can artichoke hearts, drained

⅓ cup chopped fresh parsley

12 large Iceberg lettuce leaves, to serve

The tapenade may be prepared well ahead as it keeps in a covered jar in the refrigerator for 2–3 days. Pound the olives to a paste in a mortar. Mash the anchovies with the oil from the can, then pound them into the olives. Gradually work in the capers and garlic to make a smooth paste. Add plenty of pepper and mix the lemon juice, then slowly work in the olive oil. Of course, the easiest way to make the paste is in a food processor or liquidizer; however, take care not to over-process the ingredients. Scrape all the tapenade into a small serving bowl and place it in the center of a large platter.

Trim any browned ends off the fennel, then halve the bulb lengthwise and cut it into fine slices. Thinly slice the celery. Heat the oil, then stir fry the fennel, celery and onion for 3 minutes. Add the artichoke hearts and stir fry for a further minute or so, until hot. Stir in the parsley.

Arrange the lettuce leaves on the platter around the bowl of tapenade. Divide the vegetables between the leaves and serve at once.

with the green onions. Divide this salad between four serving plates.

Drain the oil from the cheese into a large pan and heat it until quite hot – olive oil overheats quickly so this does not take long over medium to high heat. Turn the cheese into the pan and stir fry it until golden brown. Add the grapes and toss them with the cheese for a few seconds simply to warm them slightly.

Spoon the halloumi and grapes on the prepared salads and serve at once, with crusty bread to savor the cooking juices.

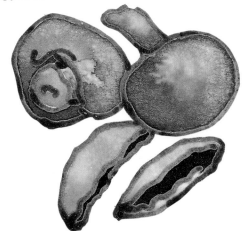

Mushroom Feast

Equally good for a light lunch as for an appetizer, sun-dried tomatoes enrich stir-fried mixed mushrooms.

SERVES 4

1 oz dried boletus	½ lb chestnut mushrooms,
mushrooms or ceps	sliced
4 sun-dried tomatoes	3 tbsp olive oil
3 tbsp port	large knob of butter
½ lb oyster mushrooms	⅓ cup snipped chives
	⅓ cup chopped fresh parsley

Place the dried mushrooms in a small saucepan with the tomatoes. Add just enough water to cover, then bring to a boil. Reduce the heat and simmer, uncovered, for 15 minutes. Drain, reserving the cooking liquor. Slice the mushrooms if necessary.

Dice the tomatoes, then mix the tomatoes and port and set aside. Strain the reserved mushroom cooking liquor through scalded cheesecloth back into the pan. Boil the liquid until it is reduced to about 3 tablespoons, then pour it over the tomatoes.

Trim any tough stalks from the oyster mushrooms. Heat the oil and butter, then stir fry the chestnut mushrooms and dried mushrooms over high heat for 1 minute. Add the oyster mushrooms and stir fry for about 2 minutes, until hot but not softened. Stir in the tomatoes with their liquid, then boil the mixture rapidly for about 30 seconds.

Finally, toss the herbs into the pan and serve the mushrooms at once, piled in individual dishes. Serve warmed crusty bread to absorb the juices.

HALLOUMI WITH GRAPES

Halloumi with Grapes

Halloumi is a tough sheeps' milk cheese of the Middle East, Turkey and Greece. Often served barbecued, the cheese forms a crisp crust on cooking and the middle softens to a pleasing texture. Serve this starter piping hot – the sweet, crisp grapes contrast deliciously with the cheese.

SERVES 4

¾ lb halloumi cheese	3 tbsp coarsely crushed
⅓ cup olive oil	coriander seeds
1 tsp dried oregano	freshly ground black pepper
1 tsp fresh thyme leaves	½ lb seedless green grapes
	1 bunch watercress
	2 green onions, chopped

Cut the cheese into ½–1 in cubes and place in a bowl. Add the olive oil, oregano, thyme, coriander and a good sprinkling of black pepper. Mix well, cover and set aside to marinate for at least an hour – the cheese may be left overnight in the refrigerator.

Remove all stalks from the grapes, then wash and dry them. Trim the leaves off the watercress and mix them

● Hot Chicken Liver Salad

This is equally good as a light lunch or for supper.

SERVES 4

½ lb chicken livers
½ tsp ground coriander
¼ tsp ground mace
¼ tsp paprika
1 tbsp all-purpose flour
salt and freshly ground black
    pepper

2 green onions, chopped
⅓ cup chopped fresh parsley
1 tsp grated lemon zest
½ lb rindless bacon slices, diced s,
3 tbsp olive oil
salad of mixed leaves, to serve
lemon wedges to garnish

Rinse, drain and dry the chicken livers on absorbent paper towels. Trim any membranes from them, then halve or quarter each piece of liver. Sprinkle the coriander, mace, paprika, flour and plenty of seasoning over the livers and mix well to coat all the pieces.

Mix the green onion with the parsley and lemon zest, then set aside. Prepare the salad bases for serving the chicken livers.

Place the bacon in a cold pan and stir fry over medium to high heat until the fat from the bacon runs.

Continue to stir fry until all the bacon pieces have become browned and are crisp. Use a slotted spoon to remove them from the pan and then drain the pieces on absorbent paper towels.

Add the olive oil to the fat remaining in the pan, heat it briefly, then add the chicken livers with all their seasonings. Stir fry until firm, lightly browned and cooked – which should take about 5 minutes. Mix in the crispy bacon and the green onion mixture. Spoon the chicken livers onto the prepared salads. Garnish the dish with lemon wedges for their juice and serve it at once, with melba toast.

TO MAKE MELBA TOAST

Lightly toast medium-thick bread slices on both sides. Cut off the crusts and slice each piece through horizontally to give two very thin slices. Toast the uncooked sides of the break well away from the heat source until lightly browned and slightly curled. Cool on a wire rack.

SIMPLY DELICIOUS MAIN DISHES

This chapter is full of ideas for everyday main meals, suitable for the family or informal suppers with friends. They are inexpensive, easy and satisfying, so guaranteed to become firm favorites. There are ideas for fish and seafood (ideal for adapting to favorite fillets or steaks), quick and easy options for poultry, and interesting ways with sausages or offal.

Flip the stir fries out on to dishes of cooked rice, pasta or salad; roll them in hot cooked pancakes; spoon them into pitta bread or slit French bread; or pile them into steaming-hot baked potatoes. In fact, treat these dishes as you would any familiar main dish and, when time is short, simply serve up chunks of crusty bread and a crunchy side salad to complete the meal.

Lemon Fish Strips with Zucchini

SERVES 4

½ lb whiting fillets or other
   firm white fish fillets, skinned
salt and freshly ground black
   pepper
¼ cup all-purpose flour
grated zest of 1 lemon
¼ cup oil

½ small onion, thinly sliced and
   separated into strips
1 red bell pepper, in thin strips
½ lb small zucchinis,
   trimmed, halved lengthwise,
   and cut in 2-in long sticks
⅓ cup snipped chives
lemon wedges to garnish

Cut the fish fillets across into ½-in wide strips. Place them in a dish, then sprinkle with the seasoning, flour and lemon zest. Mix well to coat all the fish evenly.

Heat the oil, then stir fry the onion and pepper for 3 minutes, until lightly cooked, before adding the fish. Carefully stir fry the fish, taking care not to break the strips, for 4 – 5 minutes, until lightly browned. Use a slotted spoon to transfer the fish mixture to a heated serving dish.

Add the zucchini to the oil remaining in the pan (there should be just enough to keep the pan greased) and stir fry them over high heat for about 2 minutes, so that they are hot and slightly tender. Stir in the chives, then arrange the zucchini around the fish. Garnish with lemon wedges and serve at once. The juice from the lemon should be squeezed over the fish before the fish is eaten.

COOK'S TIP

Snipped chives are cut into small pieces using scissors. Hold the washed bunch firmly in one hand and snip off the ends into a bowl.

Mackerel with White Currants

Tart white currants are a traditional accompaniment for rich, full-flavored mackerel; however, they are not usually stir fried together. Serve this summery combination with baby potatoes and fresh peas or crisp French beans.

SERVES 4

4 small to medium mackerel, gutted with heads and tails off
salt and freshly ground black pepper
⅓ cup all-purpose flour
knob of butter
1 small onion, halved and thinly sliced

½ lb white currants, topped and tailed
4 tbsp light soft brown sugar
¼ cup oil
3 tbsp chopped fresh dill or fennel
dill or fennel sprigs to garnish

Lay the mackerel one by one on a board, skin side uppermost, then run your thumb firmly along the length of the backbone. Turn the fish over and lift off the bone, starting from the tail end. The loosened backbone should lift off easily, taking the majority of the other bones with it. Pick off any remaining bones, then cut the fish across into ½-in wide strips. Coat the fish with plenty of seasoning and the flour.

Melt the butter and stir fry the onion for about 5 minutes, until lightly cooked. Add the white currants and continue to stir fry for about 3 – 4 minutes, until the fruit is lightly cooked. Add the sugar and stir fry until it melts, combining with the fruit juices in a tangy glaze. Spoon the fruit around the edge of a serving dish and keep hot.

Wipe the pan with absorbent paper towels. Heat the oil and stir fry the fish strips over medium to high heat until golden and slightly crisp at the edges. Drain the strips on absorbent paper towels and toss the dill or fennel with them. Arrange the fish on the serving dish with the white currant sauce. Garnish with dill or fennel sprigs and serve at once.

Fish with Black Beans

Serve this flavorsome Oriental-style fish dish with plain cooked rice. If it is included along with several other dishes as part of an extensive menu, the quantity of fish may be reduced by half.

SERVES 4

2 lb flounder, whiting or finnan haddle fillet, skinned
3 tbsp salted black beans
⅓ cup dry sherry
3 tbsp light soy sauce
1 tsp sesame oil
¼ cup cornstarch
3 tbsp oil

2 in piece fresh gingerroot, peeled and cut in fine strips
1 green chili, seedeed and cut into rings
1 garlic clove, crushed
1 piece lemon grass or strip of lemon zest
1 bunch green onions, cut diagonally into strips

Cut the fish across into ½-in wide strips and place these in a large shallow dish. Sprinkle the salted black beans, sherry, soy sauce and sesame oil over the fish. Cover the dish and leave the strips to marinate for 2 – 3 hours.

When you are ready to cook the fish, drain the strips well, reserving all the juices. Toss the strips in the cornstarch.

Heat the oil, then stir fry the ginger, chili, garlic and lemon grass or zest over medium heat for 4 – 5 minutes, to extract their flavor. Add the fish strips to the pan and stir fry them carefully, avoiding breaking the strips, until they are lightly browned.

Add all the green onions and continue to stir fry for 2 minutes, until the onions are cooked. Add ⅓ cup water to the reserved marinating juices and pour them into the pan. Bring to a boil over high heat, reduce the heat and stir fry for 1 minute, then serve at once.

FISH WITH BLACK BEANS

Cod with French-Style Peas

Fresh peas make this a special dish, in which case it is worth substituting chunks of monkfish for the cod; for a homely, mid-week meal opt for frozen peas and less expensive white fish. Rice, pasta, boiled or baked potatoes are all suitable accompaniments.

SERVES 4

1½ lb thick cod fillet, skinned and cut in chunks
salt and freshly ground black pepper
1 tbsp lemon juice
3 tbsp olive oil
knob of butter
1 large onion, chopped

1 garlic clove, crushed
½ cup shelled fresh peas, blanched until just tender, or frozen peas
1 Cos lettuce heart, shredded
1 tbsp chopped fresh dill or fennel
3 tbsp chopped fresh parsley
lemon or lime wedges to serve

Place the fish on a plate, season it well and sprinkle with the lemon juice. Heat the oil and butter together until the butter melts, then stir fry the onion and garlic for 5 minutes, until the onion is just beginning to soften.

Stir in the peas and stir fry them with the onion for a further 5 minutes before adding the lettuce. Continue to stir fry the vegetable mixture for 2 minutes, until the lettuce is wilted. Add the fish, dill or fennel and parsley, then stir fry gently for a further 5 minutes or until the pieces of fish are just firm. Taste and adjust the seasoning before serving with wedges of lime or lemon for their juice.

COD WITH FRENCH-STYLE PEAS

SPICY PRAWNS WITH OMELETTE

Spicy Shrimp with Omelet

SERVES 4

1 green chili, seeded and finely sliced
2 garlic cloves, crushed
1 in piece fresh gingerroot, grated
½ tsp turmeric
pinch of ground cloves
1 tbsp ground coriander
1 tbsp ground cumin
juice of 2 limes
salt and pepper

1 lb peeled cooked shrimp
⅓ cup oil
1 large onion, thinly sliced
¼ cup chopped salted peanuts
½ cup coconut milk
3 tbsp chopped fresh coriander (cilantro)

OMELET

2 eggs, beaten
½ tsp sesame oil
1 tsp oil

In a large dish, mix the chili, garlic, ginger, turmeric, cloves, ground coriander and cumin with the lime juice and plenty of seasoning. Add the shrimp and mix well to coat them all in the sauce, then cover and set aside to marinate for 2 – 3 hours. Heat the oil and stir fry the onion until it is just beginning to brown – about 10 minutes. Add the shrimp with all the marinating spices and stir fry for 5 minutes to cook the spices. Add the peanuts and coconut milk and stir until the mixture is just boiling. Taste and adjust the seasoning, then transfer to a serving dish and sprinkle with the fresh coriander (cilantro).

You will need a large flat pan for making the omelet. Beat the eggs with 3 tablespoons water and the sesame oil, adding a little seasoning. Heat the oil, pour in the eggs and cook over high heat until set and brown underneath. Use a large slice to flip the omelet over and cook the second side until browned. Cut the omelet into strips and arrange it in a criss-cross pattern on the shrimp. Serve at once.

COOK'S TIP

If you lack the confidence to flip the omelet using a slice, slide it out on to a plate, then invert it back into the pan to cook the second side.

Squid Provençal

SERVES 4

8 medium squid
⅓ cup all-purpose flour
salt and freshly ground black
  pepper
½ cup olive oil
1 onion, halved and sliced
1 green bell pepper, thinly

sliced
1–2 garlic cloves, crushed
1 bay leaf
1 lb ripe tomatoes, peeled
  and quartered
2 oz pitted black olives,
  sliced
⅓ cup chopped fresh parsley

First clean the squid (see below). Slice the body sac into rings and cut up the tentacles, if using, into small pieces. Dry the prepared squid on absorbent paper towels, then place the pieces in a basin.

Sprinkle the flour and plenty of seasoning over the squid. Heat the oil and stir fry the squid briskly until lightly browned. Use a slotted spoon to remove the pieces from the pan and drain them on absorbent paper towels.

Add the onion, pepper, garlic and bay leaf to the oil remaining in the pan. Stir fry these ingredients until the onion and pepper are slightly softened – about 5 minutes. Add the tomatoes and continue cooking, stirring all the time, for a further 5 minutes, until the tomatoes are soft but not pulpy. Add seasoning to taste and the olives, then replace the squid in the pan. Sprinkle in the parsley and stir over high heat for a minute or so. Serve with rice or plenty of crusty bread.

TO CLEAN SQUID

Pull the tentacles and head out of the body sac and it will bring with it all the innards which should be discarded. The tentacles may be cooked if liked, in which case they should be cut off just above the eyes. Discard the rest of the head. Pull out the transparent quill which is inside the body sac. Rinse the sac inside and out under cold water and rub off the mottled skin. Rinse the tentacles if using. Drain well.

Chicken with Broccoli and Cashew Nuts

SERVES 4

1 tbsp cornstarch
⅓ cup dry sherry
⅓ cup soy sauce
½ cup chicken broth
1 tsp sesame oil
3 tbsp sunflower or peanut oil

2 large boneless chicken breasts, skinned and cut into thin strips
⅓ cup unsalted cashew nuts
½ cup broccoli flowerets, broken into small pieces
7-oz can bamboo shoots, drained and sliced
6 green onions, sliced diagonally

Blend the cornstarch to a smooth thin paste with the sherry, soy sauce and broth, then set the mixture aside.

Heat the sesame and sunflower or peanut oil, then stir fry the chicken and cashew nuts until the chicken has become golden and cooked, and the nuts have been lightly browned.

Add the broccoli, bamboo shoots and green onions and continue to stir fry for 3 – 4 minutes, until the broccoli is lightly cooked.

Give the cornstarch mixture a stir, then pour it into the pan and stir over medium heat until the sauce boils. Allow the mixture to boil for a minute or so, stirring all the time, so that all the ingredients are coated in a lightly thickened sauce. Serve at once.

LEMON MARMALADE CHICKEN

Lemon Marmalade Chicken

This zesty chicken dish is extremely simple and it tastes terrific with new potatoes and a crisp salad.

SERVES 4

4 boneless chicken breasts, skinned
3 tbsp all-purpose flour
salt and freshly ground black pepper
1 tbsp sunflower oil
4 tbsp butter
1 bay leaf

1 thyme sprig
grated zest and juice of 1 large lemon
⅓ cup lemon marmalade

GARNISH (OPTIONAL)
lemon slices
thyme sprigs

Slice the chicken breasts across into large medallions, then toss the pieces in the flour and plenty of seasoning.

Heat the oil and half the butter, then stir fry the bay leaf, thyme and chicken until golden and cooked through. Add the lemon zest and juice and continue cooking, stirring all the time, for about 30 seconds to coat all the chicken with lemon.

Next add the marmalade with 3 tablespoons water and stir until the marmalade has dissolved, and has combined with the other ingredients to form a bubbling glaze. Stir in the remaining butter to give the glaze a good gloss and to enrich the dish. Serve at once, garnished with lemon slices and thyme, if wished.

CHICKEN WITH BROCCOLI AND CASHEW NUTS

TURKEY WITH CHESTNUTS AND SPROUTS

Turkey with Chestnuts and Sprouts

Chestnuts canned in brine may be substituted for the fresh ones in this recipe.

SERVES 4

1 lb chestnuts	3 tbsp oil
1½ lb Brussels sprouts	1 onion, chopped
1 lb skinned fillet of turkey	2 large sage sprigs
breast, cubed	1 thyme sprig
¼ cup all-purpose flour	1 cup chicken or turkey stock
salt and pepper	½ cup medium cider

Wash the chestnuts, then use a pointed knife to make a slit in each one. Place in a saucepan, cover with water and bring to a boil. Reduce the heat and simmer for 15 minutes. Drain and remove the chestnut shells.

Halve any large Brussels sprouts, then blanch the vegetables in boiling water for 2 minutes. Drain and set aside.

Toss the turkey with the flour and seasoning. Heat the oil, then stir fry the onion, sage and thyme for about 7 minutes, until the onion is softened. Add the turkey and continue to stir fry until all the pieces are golden and cooked. Stir in the chestnuts and Brussels sprouts, then continue to cook for 5 minutes before pouring in the stock and cider.

Stir the mixture until it boils, then stir over medium heat for 2 minutes, until the juices are thickened. Taste for seasoning before serving.

Chicken with Corn and Almonds

SERVES 4

3 boneless chicken breasts,	⅓ cup whole blanched
skinned and cut into 1-in	almonds
chunks	6 green onions, sliced diagonally
3 tbsp cornstarch	¼ cup soy sauce
1 egg white	3 tbsp lemon juice
1 tsp sesame oil	⅓ cup white wine
3 tbsp oil	1 tsp chopped gingerroot
	7 oz can corn

Place the chicken pieces in a basin. Add the cornstarch and mix well to coat all the chicken. Lightly whisk the egg white, then add it to the chicken with the sesame oil and mix well.

Heat the oil and stir fry the almonds until golden. Use a slotted spoon to remove the nuts from the pan and drain them on absorbent paper towels. Give the chicken mixture a stir, then tip it all into the oil remaining in the pan. Stir fry briskly until all the pieces are golden brown and cooked through.

Add the green onions and continue to stir fry for 2 minutes before pouring in the soy sauce, lemon juice, gingerroot and white wine. Stir in the corn and stir fry for 2 minutes, until the mixture is hot and glazed. Toss in the almonds and serve at once.

Spicy Ground Lamb with Peas

Serve this quick ground lamb dish and its cucumber raita topping with fragrant pillau rice or hot nan bread.

SERVES 4
1 lb ground lamb
3 tbsp ground coriander
1 tsp ground ginger
6 green cardamoms
2 bay leaves
juice of 1 lemon
salt and freshly ground black
   pepper
3 tbsp oil
1 onion, chopped
2 garlic cloves, crushed

1 cinnamon stick
1 tbsp cumin seeds
1 tbsp mustard seeds
1 large potato, diced
¼ lb frozen peas
⅓ cup raisins

TOPPING
¼ cucumber, peeled and diced
½ cup natural yogurt
1 tbsp chopped fresh mint
mint sprigs to garnish (optional)

Place the lamb in a bowl with the coriander, ginger, cardamoms, bay leaves and lemon juice. Add seasoning and mix thoroughly. If possible, cover and leave to marinate for several hours or even overnight in the refrigerator.

Heat the oil, then stir fry the onion, garlic, cinnamon, cumin, mustard and potato until the potato dice are browned all over. Make sure that the pan does not overheat or the spices will burn. Add the lamb mixture and continue to stir fry until the meat is browned. Stir in the peas and raisins, and then cook for a further 5 minutes. Taste for seasoning, then transfer to a heated serving dish.

For the topping, mix the cucumber and yogurt with the chopped mint, then swirl this through the spicy lamb. Garnish the dish with fresh mint, if wished, and serve at once.

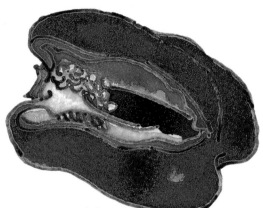

Ground Beef Creole

SERVES 4
½ lb long-grain rice
salt and black pepper
3 tbsp oil
1 large onion, thinly sliced
1 green bell pepper, seeded and
   sliced
1 red bell pepper, sliced
2 garlic cloves, crushed

450 g/1 lb lean ground
   beef steak
1 tbsp chili powder
2 × 15-oz cans chopped
   tomatoes

GARNISH
4 tomatoes, peeled and diced
¼ cup chopped fresh parsley

Cook the rice by adding it to a saucepan of boiling salted water. Bring the water back to a boil, then reduce the heat slightly and cover the pan. Simmer the rice for 15 – 20 minutes, or until tender.

Meanwhile, heat the oil and stir fry the onion, peppers and garlic for 5 minutes. Push them to one side of the pan and add the steak. Stir fry the meat briskly in the middle of the pan until evenly browned and well cooked. Add the chili and plenty of seasoning, then mix in the peppers and onion and continue to cook for 2 – 3 minutes. Pour in the tomatoes and bring the mixture to a boil, stirring all the time. Continue to cook, stirring, over medium heat for 5 – 7 minutes.

Drain the rice and transfer it to a serving dish. Ladle the beef mixture over the rice, then arrange the diced tomatoes and chopped parsley on top. Serve at once.

Sweet-Sour Pork Balls

SERVES 4

1 lb ground pork
1 tsp sesame oil
⅓ cup cornstarch
1 egg
3 tbsp soy sauce
3 tbsp oil

SWEET AND SOUR SAUCE

1 tsp cornstarch
⅓ cup dry sherry

⅓ cup soy sauce
¼ cup tomato paste
⅓ cup raw sugar
3 tbsp white wine vinegar
1 cup can pineapple chunks
   in syrup
1 large onion, cut in chunks
1 large green bell pepper,
   cut in chunks
2 carrots, cut in 1-in strips

Pound the pork with the sesame oil until well mixed, then mix in the cornstarch, egg and soy sauce in the same way. Have a plate ready to hold the pork balls. Wash, then wet your hands under cold water. Take small portions of the meat mixture, about the size of walnuts, and knead them into balls. Keep wetting your hands as this prevents the meat from sticking to them, and it gives the balls an even surface.

Before cooking the pork balls, start preparing the sauce: blend the cornstarch to a paste with ⅓ cup water. Add the sherry and soy sauce, then stir in the tomato paste, sugar and vinegar. Drain the liquid from the pineapple into the mixture.

Heat the oil and stir fry the pork balls until evenly browned and cooked through. Use a draining spoon to remove them from the pan.

Add the onion, pepper and carrots to the hot fat and stir fry these ingredients for about 5 minutes, until slightly softened. Give the liquid sauce mixture a stir, then pour it into the pan and bring to a boil, stirring all the time. Stir in the pork balls and pineapple and cook, stirring over reduced heat for 3 – 4 minutes. Serve with rice.

● Satay-flavor Pork

SERVES 4

1 lb lean boneless pork, cut in
  thin strips
3 tbsp lime or lemon juice
3 tbsp ground coriander
1 tsp ground ginger
1 garlic clove, crushed
salt and freshly ground black
  pepper
1 tsp sesame oil
⅓ cup peanut oil
1 bunch green onions, shredded

SAUCE
1 small onion, chopped

2 garlic cloves, crushed
juice of 1 lime or lemon
½ tsp chili powder
⅓ cup tahini
⅓ cup crunchy peanut butter
3 tbsp soy sauce

SALAD
½ Iceberg lettuce, shredded
½ cucumber, halved and thinly
  sliced

GARNISH
green onion curls
lime or lemon wedges

Place the pork in a bowl. Add the lime or lemon juice, coriander, ginger, garlic, seasoning and sesame oil. Stir well so that all the pieces of meat are coated in the seasoning mix. Cover and leave to marinate for several hours or overnight.

For the sauce, blend the onion, garlic, lime or lemon juice, chili and tahini to a paste in a liquidizer or food processor. Stir ¼-⅓ cup boiling water into the peanut butter to soften it to a paste, then stir in the blended mixture and the soy sauce. Add a little extra boiling water if necessary to thin the sauce.

Arrange the lettuce and cucumber on a platter or individual plates. Add the green onion curls. Heat the peanut oil and stir fry the pork until browned and cooked through. Add the green onions and stir fry for another minute. Arrange the meat on the salad base.

Spoon a little peanut sauce over the meat and green onions, then serve the rest separately. Add lime wedges to garnish and serve at once.

COOK'S TIP

Tahini is a beige-colored paste made from sesame seeds. Available from wholefood shops and oriental stores.

Pork with Orange

Pasta, rice or buckwheat are excellent accompaniments to this dish. Alternatively, the pork may be piled into slit baked potatoes, rolled in pancakes or served in taco shells.

SERVES 4

1 lb lean boneless pork	3 tbsp oil
3 sage sprigs	1 onion, halved and thinly sliced
grated zest and juice of 1 orange	½ lb carrots, cut into fine strips
3 tbsp all-purpose flour	1 tbsp clear honey
salt and freshly ground black pepper	3 tbsp dry sherry

Cut the pork across the grain into thin slices, then cut the slices into strips. Place the meat in a bowl. Discard any thick stalks from the sage, then finely shred the sprigs (the easiest way to do this is to snip them with scissors) and add them to the pork with the orange zest and juice. Mix well, then cover and leave to marinate for at least two hours. The meat may be marinated and chilled for up to 24 hours.

Use a draining spoon to remove the meat from the orange juice, pressing the strips against the side of the bowl to squeeze out as much liquid as possible. Transfer the meat to a plate or clean bowl, then sprinkle the flour and plenty of seasoning over it. Mix lightly to coat the strips.

Heat the oil, then stir fry the onion and carrots for 3 – 4 minutes. Add the meat and continue stir frying until the strips are evenly browned and cooked. Pour in the reserved marinating juices, the honey and sherry. Stir the mixture, until the juices boil and thicken slightly to coat the pork and vegetables in a shiny glaze. Serve the dish at once.

Chili Pork with Peanuts and Peaches

Good with rice, baked potatoes or in taco shells, this spicy pork and peanut mixture may be hotted up by adding extra chili, or cooled by cutting it down to a mere pinch.

SERVES 4

1 lb lean boneless pork, cut into thin strips	⅓ cup roasted peanuts
1 tsp chili powder	½ lb French beans, lightly cooked
1 tsp ground allspice	15 oz can peach slices, drained
2 cloves garlic, crushed	salt and freshly ground black pepper
2 tsp sesame oil	1 cup sour cream to serve
3 tbsp oil	
1 onion, thinly sliced	

Place the pork in a dish, then mix in the chili, allspice, garlic and sesame oil. Cover and leave to marinate for at least 2 hours or overnight in the refrigerator.

Heat the oil and stir fry the onion for 5 minutes before adding the pork. Stir fry the meat until lightly browned all over. Add the peanuts and cook for a further 2 minutes before mixing in the beans and peaches. Continue cooking for about 5 minutes, so that the beans and peaches are piping hot and the pork cooked through. Add seasoning to taste, then serve at once, offering sour cream with the spicy pork.

CHILI PORK WITH PEANUTS AND PEACHES

● Pork with Sweet Potato

This recipe is under the influence of, rather than authentic to, Caribbean cooking. I hope you like the slightly off-beat combination of the cooking method and ingredients. It's good served very simply with a refreshing salad of finely shredded celery, cucumber, green onions and pineapple, and some crusty bread; alternatively, cook up a pot of rice and red beans to make a really hearty meal.

SERVES 4

1 large sweet potato, scrubbed
1 lb lean boneless pork, finely
    diced
2 tsp ground cinnamon
freshly grated nutmeg
pinch of ground cloves or 3
    whole cloves
1 garlic clove, crushed
3 thyme sprigs

grated zest and juice of 1 lime
salt and pepper
⅓ cup peanut oil
2 green chilies, seeded and
    chopped
1 pepper, seeded and diced
1 onion, thinly sliced
2 tbsp raisins
6 tomatoes, peeled and roughly
    chopped

Cook the sweet potato in a saucepan of boiling water for 20 minutes, or until almost tender (it must not be too soft or it will break up when stir fried with the meat). Drain and cool the potato under cold water, then peel and cut it into cubes (about 1 in).

Meanwhile, place the pork in a bowl. Add the cinnamon, a good sprinkling of nutmeg, the cloves, garlic, thyme, lime zest and juice. Add some seasoning, then mix all the flavorings with the meat. If time allows, cover and set the meat aside to marinate for a couple of hours.

Heat the oil, then stir fry the meat with all the seasonings over fairly high heat until well browned. Use a slotted spoon to remove the meat from the pan. Add the chilies, pepper and onion to the oil remaining in the pan. Stir fry the vegetables over medium heat for 5 – 7 minutes, until they are beginning to soften. Add the cubes of sweet potato and continue stir frying, taking care not to break the potato, until all the sweet potato cubes are tender and thoroughly hot.

Stir in the raisins and tomatoes, replace the meat in the pan and mix well. Moisten the mixture with ⅓ cup water and continue stir frying, adding a little more water to keep the mixture juicy, but not wet. The pork should be piping hot, the raisins plump and the tomatoes pulpy, but the sweet potato should still be (just) holding its shape. Taste and adjust the seasoning before serving.

TO COOK BUCKWHEAT

Roasted buckwheat has a nutty taste. To serve 4, place 1 cup buckwheat in a saucepan and pour in 2 cups water. Add a little salt, then bring to a boil. Cover the pan tightly, reduce the heat to the lowest setting and leave 30 minutes.   Fork up the grains and serve.

PORK WITH SAUERKRAUT

Pork with Sauerkraut

Simple, yet tasty, serve this stir fry with boiled or baked potatoes or cooked buckwheat.

SERVES 4
1 lb lean boneless pork, diced
1 tsp paprika
1 garlic clove, crushed
1 tbsp caraway seeds (optional)
salt and freshly ground black
   pepper
¼ cup oil
1 onion, chopped

1 bay leaf
1 large sage sprig
2 full-flavored eating apples,
   peeled, cored and diced
1 lb sauerkraut, well drained and
   shredded
½ cup sour cream or Greek-style
   yogurt

Mix the pork, paprika, garlic, caraway (if used) and seasoning so that all the meat is well coated in the flavoring ingredients. The meat benefits from being left to marinate for a few hours (or overnight in the refrigerator), but this is not essential.

Heat the oil, then stir fry the onion, bay leaf and sage for 3 minutes. Add the pork with all the seasoning and stir fry over fairly high heat for 5 minutes. Add the apples, then continue to stir fry until the pork is well cooked and browned. Add the sauerkraut and stir fry for a few minutes to heat the vegetable through.

When the sauerkraut is piping hot, stir in the sour cream or yogurt to moisten the mixture. Taste and adjust the seasoning and stir for a few seconds, but do not overcook as the sour cream or yogurt will curdle.

Smoked Sausage Succotash

This is a quick variation of the American stew of beans and corn.

SERVES 4
knob of butter
1 small onion, finely chopped
¾ lb smoked pork sausage, sliced
½ lb frozen corn
2 × 15 oz cans lima beans

3 ripe tomatoes, peeled, seeded
   and diced
⅔ cup half-and-half
salt and pepper
3 tbsp chopped fresh parsley

Melt the butter, then stir fry the onion and sausage together until the sausage is lightly browned and succulent, and the onion softened – about 8 minutes.

Add the corn and lima beans. Continue stir frying for 5 minutes, or until the corn is thawed and cooked. Lastly stir in the tomatoes and cook for 1 minute before pouring in the half-and-half and adding a little seasoning. Heat gently but do not allow to boil or the half-and-half will curdle. Taste for seasoning, then sprinkle in the parsley and serve.

SAUSAGE STIR-ABOUT

Sausage Stir-About

This tasty mixture is good in baked potatoes, taco shells, rolled in pancakes or stuffed into warmed split pitta bread. The dish can be topped with natural yoghurt or sour cream if you like.

SERVES 4

½ lb pork sausagemeat	salt and pepper
1 cup fresh breadcrumbs	⅓ cup oil
1 onion, grated	1 lb potatoes, diced
⅜ cup ready-to-eat dried apricots, chopped	½ lb cut green beans, cooked until just tender
1 tsp dried marjoram or oregano	lots of chopped fresh parsley

Mix the sausagemeat, breadcrumbs, onion, apricots, marjoram or oregano and seasoning until thoroughly combined. Use two spoons to separate the mixture into small lumps about the size of walnuts – there is no need to be too fussy about shape as the meat will break up during cooking.

    Heat the oil and stir fry the potatoes until they are crisp and golden brown, controlling the heat carefully to prevent the oil from overheating. Add the lumps of sausagemeat and continue stir frying over medium heat until all the meat is well cooked. Add the beans and stir fry for 3 – 5 minutes, until they are piping hot. Sprinkle in lots of parsley and serve at once.

Chili Franks

A quick, tasty dish to serve with rice or baked potatoes. Use good-quality frankfurters for best results, and adjust the number of chilies according to personal preference and their type – if using mild chilies, then add four; if using very hot ones, then two will be sufficient.

SERVES 4

3 tbsp oil	on size), sliced
1 large onion, chopped	1 tbsp ground cumin
2 garlic cloves, crushed	1 tbsp dried marjoram
2 – 4 green chilies, seeded and chopped	salt and freshly ground black pepper
1 green bell pepper, seeded and chopped	2 × 15 oz cans red kidney beans, drained
8 – 12 frankfurters (depending	2 × 15 oz cans chopped tomatoes

Heat the oil, then stir fry the onion, garlic, chilies and pepper for 4 – 5 minutes, until softened slightly. Add the frankfurters and continue to stir fry for about 10 minutes, or until the sausage slices are browned.

    Stir in the cumin, marjoram and seasoning, and cook for 1 minute before tipping in the kidney beans and tomatoes. Stir well and bring to a boil, then simmer the mixture for 3 minutes, continuing to stir all the time, before serving.

GAMMON WITH CAULIFLOWER

Cured Ham with Cauliflower

A good recipe for inexpensive ham offcuts or for corner gammon.

SERVES 4

1 small cauliflower, trimmed and broken into small flowerets	1 tbsp fennel seeds (optional)
	3 tbsp oil
1 lb cured ham, trimmed and cut into large dice	1 large onion, chopped
	1 bay leaf
3 tbsp all-purpose flour	2 large sage sprigs
freshly ground black pepper	1 cup unsweetened apple juice

Plunge the cauliflower into a large saucepan of boiling water. Bring the water back to a boil, cook for 1 minute, then drain the flowerets and set them aside.

Toss the ham with the flour, plenty of pepper and the fennel seeds, if using. Heat the oil, add the ham and any loose flour. Stir fry for 1 minute, then add the onion, bay leaf and sage. Continue to cook until the diced ham is evenly browned and cooked through. Add the cauliflower and stir fry for a further 3 minutes.

Pour in the apple juice and bring the sauce to a boil, stirring all the time. Cook for 2 – 3 minutes, then serve the dish at once.

Piquant Kidneys

SERVES 4

⅓ cup dry sherry	salt and freshly ground black pepper
1 tbsp Dijon mustard	3 tbsp oil
dash of Worcestershire sauce	¼ lb rindless bacon slices, chopped
1 tbsp capers, chopped	1 onion, finely chopped
1 lb lambs' kidneys, halved and cored	¼ lb button mushrooms, halved
⅓ cup all-purpose flour	⅓ cup natural yogurt
½ tsp ground mace	chopped fresh parsley to serve
½ tsp dried thyme	

Mix the sherry, mustard, Worcestershire sauce and capers and set aside. Toss the kidneys in the flour, mace, thyme and seasoning, insuring they are evenly coated.

Heat the oil, then stir fry the bacon and onion for about 8 minutes, unitl the bacon is browned and the onion softened. Add the kidneys and stir fry briskly for about 6 minutes, until they are sealed and browned. Tip the mushrooms into the pan and continue stir frying for a further 5 minutes. Lastly add the sherry mixture. Cook, stirring slightly less vigorously, until the juices are bubbling hot and the kidneys are cooked through.

Transfer the kidney mixture to serving plates and top each portion with a little yogurt and plenty of parsley.

● Paprika Liver

Serve this liver with sweet bell peppers on a bed of cooked noodles and offer a crisp green salad as an accompaniment.

SERVES 4

¾ lb lambs' liver, cut in strips
⅓ cup all-purpose flour
1 tbsp paprika
salt and freshly ground black pepper
knob of butter
3 tbsp oil
1 garlic clove, crushed
1 onion, thinly sliced

1 red bell pepper, seeded and thinly sliced
1 green bell pepper, seeded and thinly sliced
½ cup chicken broth
425 g can chopped tomatoes
12 pimento-stuffed green olives, sliced

Toss the liver with the flour, paprika and plenty of seasoning. Heat the butter and oil, then stir fry the garlic, onion and peppers for 8 minutes, or until softened. Push this mixture to one side of the pan and stir fry the liver strips fairly briskly, until evenly browned and just cooked.

Pour in the broth and tomatoes and bring to a boil, stirring frequently. Simmer for 5 minutes, stirring occasionally. Taste for seasoning and then add the stuffed olives to the dish.

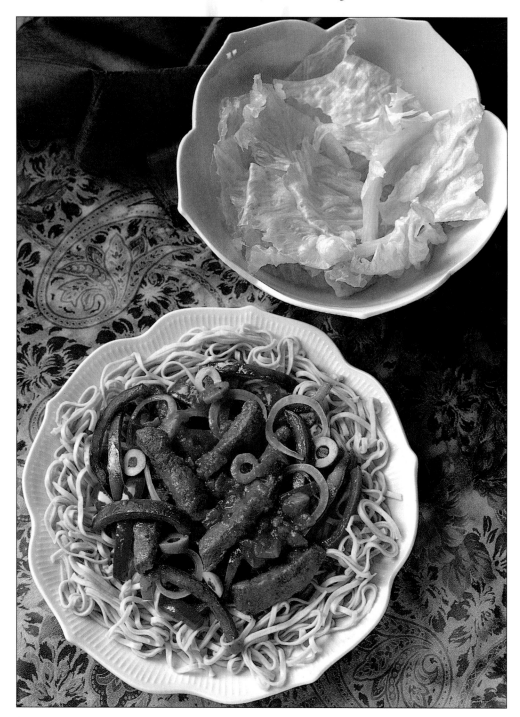

FLAGEOLET BEANS WITH SPINACH

Flageolet Beans with Spinach

This no-fuss, no-meat main course is ideal for summer days when spare time is best spent outdoors rather than slaving for hours in a hot kitchen.

SERVES 4

1 lb fresh spinach, trimmed and washed
knob of butter
3 tbsp olive oil
6 green onions, chopped
2 × 15 oz cans flageolet beans, drained
2 small zucchini, trimmed and thinly sliced
3 tbsp chopped fresh mint
several large basil sprigs, leaves shredded
½ lb feta cheese, crumbled
salt and freshly ground black pepper

Press all the spinach leaves into a large saucepan while still dripping wet. Put a lid on the pan and place it over high heat. Cook, shaking the pan often, for about 5 minutes, or until the spinach has wilted and shrunk. Stir the leaves, cover and cook for a further 2 minutes or so, until tender. Drain well, then replace the spinach in the pan and add the knob of butter. Cover and leave over low heat to keep hot.

Heat the oil, then stir fry the green onions, flageolet beans and zucchini for 5 minutes, until the zucchini are just cooked. Spoon the spinach on to one large or four individual serving plates. Toss the mint, basil and feta into the vegetables, and add seasoning to taste. Spoon the vegetables over the spinach and then serve the dish at once.

Sultan's Liver

SERVES 4

1 cup roasted buckwheat, cooked (see page 000)
1 small eggplant, trimmed and cut in small cubes
salt and freshly ground black pepper
⅓ cup olive oil
¾ lb lambs' liver, cut in thin strips
2 garlic cloves, crushed
4 cloves
1 cinnamon stick
¼ cup pine nuts
⅓ cup white raisins
2 tsp dried oregano
1 lb tomatoes, peeled, seeded and quartered .

Cook the buckwheat, cover it and set aside ready for serving. Meanwhile, place the eggplant cubes in a colander or strainer and sprinkle them with salt. Place over a bowl and leave to drain for 15 minutes, then rinse and pat dry on absorbent paper towels.

Heat the oil, then stir fry the liver strips, garlic, cloves and cinnamon stick until just firm – about 3 minutes. Add the eggplant, pine nuts, white raisins, oregano and seasoning, then continue to stir fry until the liver is cooked and the eggplant is just cooked but not soft.

Finally, stir in the tomatoes and continue to cook, stirring, for 5 minutes until all the ingredients are cooked and the flavors well combined.

Fork the buckwheat and place on one large or four individual serving dishes. Divide the liver mixture between them and serve at once.

A MEAL IN A PAN

This chapter includes a broad selection of recipes
that are satisfying and balanced enough to form a
complete main course. They range from dishes such
as Fishballs with Noodles or Minted Lamb with
Lentils, which are suitable for informal meals with
friends, to Sprouts with Salami or Bread and Bacon
Supper, which are ideal mid-week suppers.

Although they are sufficient alone, a fresh side
salad always complements a one-pot main dish and
some warm bread – whether pitta, nan, white or
wholewheat – is an acceptable offering for scooping
up the last of the cooking juices.

If you are cooking for more than two, then make
sure you have a good sized pan – a skillet or sauté
pan if not a wok – to hold all the ingredients. Take the
pan to the table or go for informal bowls as serving
vessels. If you find them comfortable to use,
remember that chopsticks are ideal for eating many
mixed dishes as well as Chinese specialities.

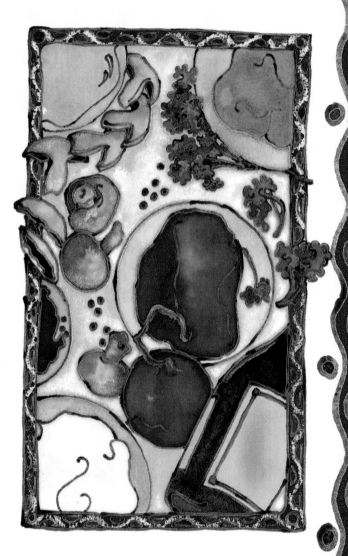

GOLDEN FISH WITH POTATOES

● Golden Fish with Potatoes

SERVES 4

⅓ cup all-purpose flour	¼ cup oil
½ tsp turmeric	2 celery stalks, thinly sliced
salt and freshly ground white pepper	1 small onion, finely chopped
grated zest of 1 lemon	½ lb French beans, blanched in boiling water for 1 minute and drained
1 lb monkfish, thick cod fillet or other firm white fish, skinned and cubed	1½ lb baby potatoes, scraped and cooked

Mix the flour, turmeric, seasoning and lemon zest, then toss the fish cubes in this mixture to coat them completely.

Heat the oil, then stir fry the celery and onion until slightly softened, about 7 minutes. Add the beans and potatoes and continue to stir fry for 5 – 7 minutes, until all the vegetables are hot and tender.

Push the vegetables to one side of the pan and add the fish. Stir fry the cubes over medium to high heat, taking care not to break them, until golden brown. Gently mix the ingredients and serve at once.

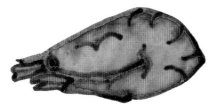

● Fishballs with Noodles

SERVES 4

1 lb white fish, skinned and cut in chunks	1 piece lemon grass or strip of lemon zest
¼ cup cornstarch	1 celery stalk, cut diagonally into thin slices
1 egg white	1 bunch green onions, sliced
salt and freshly ground white pepper	¼ lb snow peas, trimmed
¾ cup Chinese egg noodles	¼ cup soy sauce
¼ cup oil	¼ cup dry sherry
4 thin slices fresh gingerroot	

Pound the fish with the cornstarch until it is reduced to a paste, then work in the egg white and seasoning. Wet your hands and shape the mixture into small balls, kneading it together so that the fish binds well.

Place the noodles in the pan and pour in enough boiling water to cover them. Bring back to a boil and cook for 2 minutes, then drain the noodles and set aside.

Heat the oil, then stir fry the ginger and lemon grass or lemon zest for 1 minute before adding the fish balls. Stir fry the fish balls until firm and lightly browned. Add the celery, green onions and snow peas, and continue to stir fry for 5 – 8 minutes, or until the vegetables are slightly tender but not soft.

Add the noodles, soy sauce and sherry, and stir the mixture over high heat until the noodles are hot. Serve the dish at once.

◗ Szechuan Noodles

SERVES 4

¾ lb Chinese egg noodles

1 tbsp cornstarch

3 tbsp dry sherry

⅓ cup chicken broth

⅓ cup light soy sauce

⅓ cup oil

2 green chilies, seeded and
chopped

2 garlic cloves, crushed

2-in piece fresh gingerroot,
peeled
and cut into fine strips

½ lb lean boneless pork, cut into
fine strips

1 red bell pepper, seeded and cut
into fine, short strips

1 bunch green onions, cut
diagonally into fine slices

7 oz can bamboo shoots, drained
and cut in strips

1-in slice Chinese cabbage head,
separated into pieces

Place the noodles in the pan and pour in enough boiling water to cover them. Bring back to a boil and cook for 2 minutes, then drain the noodles. While the noodles are cooking, blend the cornstarch with the sherry, broth and soy sauce, then set aside.

Wipe the pan and heat the oil. Add the noodles, spreading them out thinly, and fry over medium to high heat until they are crisp and golden underneath, patting them down slightly into a thin cake – they will set more or less in shape. Use a large slice to turn the noodles over and brown the second side. Don't worry if the noodles break up slightly – the aim is to end up with some that are crisp and others that remain soft. Transfer the noodles to a large serving dish and keep hot.

Add the chilies, garlic, ginger and pork to the oil remaining in the pan. Stir fry the mixture over high heat until the pork is browned. Add the pepper and green onions and stir fry for a further 2 minutes before adding the bamboo shoots. Stir fry for 1 minute to heat the bamboo shoots.

Give the cornstarch mixture a stir and pour it into the pan. Bring to a boil, stirring, and cook over high heat for 30 seconds. Mix in the Chinese cabbage, stir for less than a minute to heat the cabbage. Spoon the pork mixture over the noodles and serve at once.

● Lamb with Garbanzo Beans

Lamb and garbanzo beans are natural partners flavorwise, and crunchy, aromatic fennel adds a bit of "zing" to one of my favorite meals in a pan.

SERVES 4

salt and freshly ground black pepper
¾ lb lean boneless lamb, cut into fine strips (leg steaks or fillet are ideal)
freshly grated nutmeg
1 tsp dried oregano
3 rosemary sprigs
1 garlic clove, crushed (optional)

½ cup red wine (use a full-bodied one if possible)
¼ cup olive oil
1 small onion, halved and thinly sliced
2 fennel bulbs, thinly sliced
2 × 15 oz cans garbanzo beans, drained
2 tsp arrowroot

Season the lamb well, then mix in a good sprinkling of nutmeg, the oregano, rosemary and garlic, if used. Pour in the wine, cover and leave to marinate for a couple of hours or longer if possible (overnight if time allows).

Heat the oil and stir fry the onion for 5 minutes. Use a slotted spoon to add the lamb to the pan, reserving the marinating liquid. Stir fry the meat over fairly high heat until all the strips are browned. Add the fennel and continue stir frying for about 10 minutes, reducing the heat to prevent the meat from overcooking. The fennel should be slightly tender but not softened.

Add the garbanzo beans and stir fry for 2–3 minutes to heat them through. Pour in the reserved marinade and bring to a boil, stirring. Simmer for 2 minutes.

Blend the arrowroot with ⅓ cup water, then add it to the pan and stir over medium heat until the liquid boils to form a thin glaze for the ingredients. Remove the pan from the heat at once, or switch the heat off, as the arrowroot thickening will thin down if it is allowed to simmer. Taste for seasoning and serve with chunks of crusty bread to mop up the juices.

Chicken Balls with Rice Sticks

I first made this when I had been rather overgenerous in preparing chicken balls for a Japanese meal. The leftovers made a terrific stir fry with ribbon rice sticks, snow peas, cucumber and a variety of other leftover prepared ingredients.

SERVES 4

3 boneless chicken breasts, skinned and ground
⅓ cup all-purpose flour
¼ cup sake or dry sherry
6 tbsp soy sauce (use Japanese sauce if possible)
1 small egg
1 bunch green onions
salt and pepper

2 tsp sugar
½ lb ribbon rice sticks
¼ cup peanut oil
2 small carrots, cut lengthwise into very thin strips
½ lb snow peas, trimmed
½ cucumber, peeled, halved crosswise and thinly sliced lengthwise

A food processor is ideal for grinding the raw chicken, otherwise it may be done by hand using a chef's large knife and a chopping action: eventually the chicken will progress from being chopped in fine dice into a fine, almost ground, mixture.

Mix the flour with the chicken, pounding the mixture well. Add 1 tablespoon each of the sake or dry sherry and soy sauce, then mix in the egg. Finely chop the white parts from 2 green onions, then add them to the mixture with the seasoning. When all the ingredients are thoroughly combined the mixture may seem a little soft, but don't worry – if it is too firm at this stage the cooked balls will be slightly tough in texture. Cover the mixture and chill it on a low shelf in the refrigerator for 30 minutes, or put it in the freezer for about 15 minutes.

Heat the remaining sake and soy sauce with the sugar, stirring, then bring the mixture to a boil and boil hard for 1 minute, set aside. It is best to do this in a saucepan but you can use your stir fry pan, then pour the mixture into a large bowl, making sure you scrape it all out of the pan by using a plastic spatula. In a wide pan 1 minute's cooking may be too long as the liquid evaporates more speedily.

Slice the remaining green onions diagonally. Place the rice sticks in the pan and pour in boiling water to cover them. Bring to a boil and cook for 1 – 2 minutes, until just soft. Drain and rinse under cold water.

Wet your hands and shape the chicken mixture into balls, slightly smaller than walnuts – they do not have to be perfect in shape, but if you keep your hands well wetted with cold water the mixture is easier to shape.

Heat the oil and stir fry the chicken balls over medium to high heat, until they are golden brown all over. At first they should be coaxed and stirred around the pan gently until the mixture firms. If they are stirred smoothly and constantly they will form neat balls. Then they may be stir fried with more vigour so that they brown evenly and cook through. Use a slotted spoon to remove the chicken balls from the pan, adding them to the boiled soy sauce mixture. Toss the balls in the sauce to coat them completely.

Add the carrots, snow peas and green onions to the oil remaining in the pan and stir fry the vegetables for about 3 minutes before adding the cucumber. Continue stir frying for about 2 minutes, until the vegetables are just cooked and piping hot. Now, toss in the rice sticks (you may have to rinse them quickly under cold water if they have set in a block – shake off excess water) and stir fry them for a minute or so to heat them up. Replace the chicken balls in the pan and mix well, then serve.

Sprouts with Salami

SERVES 4

3 tbsp tomato paste
⅓ cup red wine
3 tbsp oil
1 lb Brussels sprouts, halved
1 small onion, halved and thinly sliced
1 green bell pepper, seeded and thinly sliced
2 bay leaves

salt and freshly ground black pepper
¼ lb salami, cut into fine strips (use good-quality Italian salami for best results)
2 × 15-oz cans borlotti beans, drained

Mix the tomato paste with the wine and 2 – 3 tablespoons of water to make a slightly thickened glaze for adding at the end of stir frying.

Heat the oil, then stir fry the sprouts, onion, pepper and bay leaves with some seasoning over medium heat for 10 minutes, until the sprouts are slightly tender. Add the salami, increase the heat and stir fry for a further 2 minutes before adding the borlotti beans and tomato glaze. Stir for another 2 – 3 minutes or so, until the beans are hot and the mixture is moist with bubbling glaze. Taste for seasoning before serving – open-textured, flat and floury Italian bread is an excellent accompaniment when available.

SPROUTS WITH SALAMI

🔴 Mustard Rabbit

This is a good everyday dish, but healthwise it is best to reserve the generous use of butter for frying the bread as an occasional treat.

SERVES 4

1 short French loaf, sliced (see method)	⅓ cup mild wholegrain mustard
⅓ cup olive oil	salt and freshly ground black pepper
4 tbsp butter	¼ cup oil
plenty of chopped fresh parsley	2 lb potatoes, cut in large dice
3 tbsp chopped fresh mint (optional)	½ lb pickling onions
1 lb boneless rabbit meat, cut into small cubes	1 carrot, diced
	½ lb shelled peas (blanched fresh or frozen)
1 tbsp all-purpose flour	1 cup chicken broth

The French bread slices should not be too thin nor too thick – just under 1 in. Discard the end pieces. Heat the oil and butter, then quickly toss all the bread slices into the pan and stir fry them until crisp and golden. Do not leave the slices to sit in the oil and butter or they will absorb the fat unevenly, leaving some slices dry. Toss the parsley and mint, if used, into the pan and mix the herbs with the bread. Set the bread aside.

Coat the rabbit cubes with flour, then mix in the mustard and seasoning to coat all the pieces evenly. Heat the oil and stir fry the potatoes for 5 minutes. Add the onions and carrot, then continue stir frying until the potatoes are lightly browned and the onions are just tender. Add the rabbit and continue stir frying until all the pieces are lightly browned.

Stir in the peas and cook for a couple of minutes if they are frozen, before pouring in the stock. Bring to a boil, stirring, so that the mustard from the meat thickens the liquid slightly. Cook at a rapid simmer for 2 – 3 minutes, then taste and adjust the seasoning before serving in individual dishes or bowls. Garnish with some of the French bread and offer the rest separately.

Egg-Fried Rice with Shrimp

Crunchy water chestnuts add a pleasing contrast in texture to this favorite rice dish.

SERVES 4

1 cup long-grain rice, cooked
¼ cup oil
1 tsp sesame oil
1 bunch green onions, shredded
   diagonally
7 oz can water chestnuts,

drained and sliced
¼ lb frozen peas
¾ lb peeled cooked shrimp
3 eggs, beaten
¼ cup light soy sauce
whole cooked shrimp to garnish

The rice should be freshly cooked. Heat the oils together, then stir fry the onions, water chestnuts and peas for 3–5 minutes, until the peas are thawed and hot. Add the shrimp and stir fry for another minute.

Lower the heat, pour the eggs into the pan and cook until they are half set. They should be thickened, but not scrambled – if they are too thin, they coat the rice grains too freely and give the finished rice an inferior texture. If the eggs are allowed to set before the rice is added, they tend to be overcooked and slightly rubbery in the finished dish.

Tip all the rice into the pan and turn it over in the egg mixture to combine all the ingredients evenly. The eggs should finish cooking almost immediately if the rice is hot. Sprinkle in the soy sauce and serve at once, garnished with the whole shrimp, if liked.

Five-Spice Pork with Noodles

SERVES 4

1 lb lean boneless pork, cut in thin
  slices
½ tsp five-spice powder
salt and freshly ground black
  pepper
2 green onions, finely chopped
1 garlic clove, crushed

½ lb Chinese egg noodles
⅓ cup peanut oil
8 oz can bamboo shoots, sliced
½ lb snow peas, trimmed
¼ cup soy sauce
3 tbsp roasted sesame seeds

Mix the pork with the five-spice powder, seasoning, green onions and garlic. Cover and leave to marinate for at least an hour or as long as overnight.

Cover the noodles with boiling water and bring back to a boil. Cook for 2 minutes, then drain and rinse under cold water.

Heat the oil and stir fry the pork until well browned. Add the bamboo shoots and snow peas, and continue to stir fry for 3 – 4 minutes, or until the vegetables are cooked. Push the meat mixture to one side of the pan or make a space in the middle and add the noodles. Stir the noodles for 2 minutes to heat them through, then stir in the other ingredients, soy sauce and sesame seeds. Cook for 1 minute before serving.

FIVE-SPICE PORK WITH NOODLES

Rice with Pork and Peppers

SERVES 4

¼ cup oil
1 large onion, thinly sliced
¾ lb lean boneless pork, cut in
  thin strips
1 red bell pepper, seeded and
  thinly sliced
1 green bell pepper, seeded and
  thinly sliced

salt and freshly ground black
  pepper
a little grated nutmeg
grated zest of 1 orange
¼ lb long-grain rice, freshly
  cooked
¼ lb wild rice, freshly cooked

Heat the oil and stir fry the onion for 2 minutes before adding the pork. Stir fry the meat and onion together until the meat is cooked through and lightly browned, keeping the heat fairly high to seal the strips of meat. Add the peppers, seasoning, nutmeg and orange zest. Reduce the heat slightly and stir fry for 3 – 5 minutes, or until the peppers are cooked.

Stir in both types of rice and cook for a few minutes so that the ingredients are well combined. If the rice has been allowed to cool, it should be reheated thoroughly at this stage – the result is best if the rice is freshly cooked and piping hot when added to the pan.

Lentils with Mushrooms and Almonds

A delicious vegetarian main course, this is an ideal mid-week feast as a change from meat-based main dishes.

SERVES 4

½ lb green lentils, cooked
1 lb button mushrooms, sliced
1 tsp ground mace
salt and pepper
⅓ cup olive oil
½ cup blanched almonds, split in half
knob of butter
½ lb oyster mushrooms
⅓ cup snipped chives

The lentils should be freshly cooked, drained and set aside in a covered pan so that they stay hot while the mushrooms are stir fried.

Mix the mushrooms with the mace and plenty of seasoning. Heat the oil and stir fry the mushrooms briskly until they begin to brown. When they give up their juices, continue stir frying until all the liquid has evaporated and the mushrooms are greatly reduced in volume. At this stage they have a good, concentrated flavor; they should be dark in color and the majority of the liquid in the pan should be the remainder of the oil in which they have cooked.

Use a slotted spoon to remove the mushrooms from the pan and add them to the lentils. Cover and set aside. Stir fry the almonds in the oil remaining in the pan until they are golden, then add them to the lentils. Fork the almonds and mushrooms into the lentils, then transfer the mixture to a serving dish or individual bowls.

Melt the butter in the pan and stir fry the oyster mushrooms over fairly high heat for a minute or so – they should be very lightly cooked. If the mushrooms are overcooked they will collapse. Stir in the chives with a little seasoning and spoon the mixture over the lentils, scraping any juices from the cooking pan. Serve at once.

Minted Lamb with Vegetables

SERVES 4

1 lb lean boneless lamb, diced
3 tbsp all-purpose flour
salt and freshly ground black
    pepper
3 tbsp oil
knob of butter
½ lb small pickling onions

1½ lb baby potatoes, boiled until
    tender
½ lb snow peas
1 cup dry white wine
⅓ cup chopped fresh mint
1 head chicory, roughly
    shredded, to serve
mint sprigs to garnish

Toss the lamb with the flour and seasoning. Heat the oil
and butter, then stir fry the onions for about 10 minutes,
until they are lightly browned. Add the meat and stir fry
for a further 8 – 10 minutes, until both meat and onions
are browned and the onions are tender.

Stir in the potatoes and snow peas and continue to
stir fry for 5 minutes or so, until the potatoes are hot
and the snow peas are lightly cooked. Pour in the wine
and bring to a boil. Boil rapidly, stirring, for 2 minutes, so
that the ingredients are coated in a lightly thickened
glaze. Taste and adjust the seasoning.

Stir in the mint just before turning the lamb mixture
out on to a bed of chicory, either on one large dish or on
individual plates. Garnish the dish with mint sprigs.

Sesame Garbanzo Beans with Chicken

Transform leftover cooked chicken into a tasty meal. In
fact this recipe may be used for any cooked meat

SERVES 4

1 lettuce heart, shredded
2-in piece cucumber, peeled and
    diced
1 bunch radishes, sliced
3 tbsp roasted sesame seeds
⅓ cup olive oil
2 × 15 oz cans garbanzo beans,
    drained
1 lb cooked chicken, diced

½ cup tahini
⅓ cup snipped chives
3 tbsp chopped fresh parsley
salt and freshly ground black
    pepper
2 avocados, halved, pitted,
    peeled and cut in chunks
½ cup pitted black olives, halved
1 lemon, cut into wedges

Mix the lettuce, cucumber, radishes and sesame seeds,
then arrange this salad around the edge of four serving
plates or one large dish.

Heat the oil, then stir fry the garbanzo beans and
chicken for about 5 minutes, or until the chicken is
thoroughly heated. Stir in the tahini until it combines
with the oil to coat the ingredients in a creamy dressing.
Add the herbs, seasoning and avocados, then stir the
black olives into the mixture.

Divide the chicken mixture between the serving
plates and garnish with lemon wedges. The lemon juice
should be squeezed over the chicken mixture and salad.

Pork-Filled Taco Shells

SERVES 4

3 tbsp oil
1 onion, chopped
1 green bell pepper, seeded and diced
2 celery stalks, thinly sliced
½ lb ground pork
salt
¼ tsp cayenne pepper
15 oz can red kidney beans, drained
15 oz can chopped tomatoes
Tabasco sauce to taste
2 avocados, halved, pitted and diced
grated zest and juice of 1 lime
8 taco shells
shredded lettuce to serve

Heat the oil, then stir fry the onion, pepper and celery until softened before adding the pork to the pan. Sprinkle in salt and the cayenne pepper, then stir fry the meat until it is cooked and well-browned.

Add the kidney beans and tomatoes, then stir fry for a further 5 minutes. Lastly, add Tabasco sauce to taste and remove the pan from the heat.

Toss the avocados with the lime zest and juice. Spoon some of the meat mixture into each taco shell and top with avocado. Arrange the filled shells supported on a bed of shredded lettuce and serve at once.

Bacon with Eggplant and Walnuts

SERVES 4

2 large eggplant, trimmed and cubed
salt and freshly ground black pepper
½ cup olive oil
3 leeks, thinly sliced
½ lb rindless bacon slices, roughly chopped
⅔ cup walnut pieces
½ lb small mushrooms, halved
plenty of chopped fresh parsley or shredded basil leaves

Place the eggplant in a colander, sprinkle them with salt and set aside over a bowl for 15 minutes. Rinse well and pat dry on absorbent paper towels.

Heat the oil and stir fry the leeks for 5 minutes until softened. Add the eggplant pieces and continue stir frying until they are lightly browned on the outside, and tender but not soft. Stir in the bacon and walnuts, then continue cooking until the bacon is cooked and the eggplant pieces are softened.

Add the mushrooms with seasoning and stir fry for a further 3 minutes, to heat the mushrooms through without overcooking them. Taste for seasoning before serving sprinkled with parsley or basil. Wholegrain rolls or pitta bread are ideal accompaniments.

Tofu Chow Mein

SERVES 4

4 large dried Chinese mushrooms
⅓ cup soy sauce
3 tbsp dry sherry
1 garlic clove, crushed
¼ tsp five spice powder
½ lb tofu, cubed
2 tsp cornstarch
½ lb Chinese egg noodles

¼ cup peanut oil
1 small carrot, cut into matchstick strips
1 yellow bell pepper, cut into short thin strips
6 green onions, sliced diagonally
7-oz can water chestnuts, drained and sliced
½ lb bean sprouts

Place the dried mushrooms in a small bowl or mug and pour in just enough hot water to cover them. Use a saucer or base of a second mug to press the mushrooms down and keep them submerged. Leave to soak for 20 minutes.

Mix the soy sauce, sherry, garlic and five spice powder, then pour this mixture over the tofu and set aside.

Drain the mushrooms, reserving the liquid. Discard their tough stalks, then slice the caps. Blend the cornstarch to a paste with the soaking liquid.

Place the noodles in the pan and pour in boiling water to cover them. Bring to a boil and cook for 2 minutes, then drain and spread out on a heated serving dish. Cover with foil and keep hot.

Heat the oil. Drain any liquid from the tofu into the cornstarch liquid, then stir fry the tofu over high heat until golden all over. Take care at first not to break the pieces – once the tofu is crisp outside it is less likely to break up.

Add the carrot, pepper, mushrooms and green onions and stir fry until the vegetables are slightly softened. Add the water chestnuts and continue to stir fry for 2 minutes, or until hot.

Give the cornstarch liquid a stir and pour it into the pan. Bring to a boil, stirring, and simmer for 1 minute. Add the bean sprouts and cook, stirring for 1 minute, to heat them. Pour the mixture over the noodles and serve the dish at once.

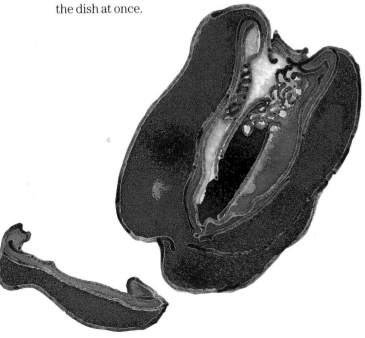

Curried Pork with Beans

The quality of the curry powder determines the flavor of the finished dish – buy a reputable brand or mix your own spices.

SERVES 4

1 lb lean boneless pork, diced
¼ cup oil or ghee
1 large onion, thinly sliced
2 × 15 oz cans red kidney beans, drained
¼ cup chopped coriander (cilantro) leaves

MARINADE

salt and freshly ground black pepper
1 tbsp curry powder
1 in piece fresh gingerroot, finely grated
1 onion, grated
2 garlic cloves, crushed
1 tbsp tomato paste
juice of 1 lemon
¼ cup natural yogurt

Place the meat in a dish and add all the marinade ingredients. Mix well, then cover and leave the pork to marinate overnight.

Drain the meat well, reserving the marinade. Heat the oil or ghee, then stir fry the onion for about 15 minutes, or until lightly browned. Add the meat and continue stir frying until all the pieces are cooked. Stir in the kidney beans and pour in any reserved marinade, then continue to cook, stirring, for 15 minutes. Serve at once, sprinkled with fresh coriander (cilantro).

CURRIED PORK WITH BEANS

Vegetable Pancakes

If you do not want to make pancakes, the stir fried vegetables may be served in pitta bread, as a topping for baked potatoes or in a split baguette. They can, of course, be served quite simply by themselves with a couple of slices of wholegrain bread to fill hungry diners!

SERVES 4

2 carrots, cut into strips
2 leeks, cut into short thin strips
½ celeriac, cut into strips
1 red or yellow bell pepper, seeded and cut into short thin strips
1 cup medium cider
¼ lb ready-to-eat dried apricots, sliced
2 large tarragon sprigs, leaves removed
1 bay leaf

3 tbsp olive oil
½ cup slivered almonds
2 zucchini, cut into short thin strips
6 oz soft cheese with garlic and herbs

PANCAKES

good ¾ cup wholewheat flour
salt and pepper
2 eggs
1⅓ cups milk
1 tbsp oil plus oil for cooking

Combine the carrots, leeks, celeriac and pepper with the cider, apricots, tarragon leaves and bay leaf in a dish. Cover and set aside to marinate.

Next make the pancakes: turn the flour into a bowl and mix in a little seasoning. Make a well in the middle, then add the eggs and some of the milk. Gradually beat the eggs and milk into the flour to make a smooth batter, adding more milk as the mixture thickens. Beat well until smooth. If possible set aside for 20 minutes before cooking. Stir in 1 tablespoon oil before frying the batter to make eight large thin pancakes. If the batter thickens on standing, add a little water.

Layer the cooked pancakes with pieces of absorbent paper towels to prevent them sticking together, and cover the stack with foil. Keep them hot.

Drain the vegetables and apricots, reserving the liquid. Heat the olive oil and stir fry the almonds until lightly browned. Add the drained vegetables and apricots, and stir fry until the leek and celeriac are just tender. Add the zucchini and stir fry for 3 – 5 minutes before pouring in the reserved cider marinade with seasoning to taste.

Bring the cooking liquid to a boil, then stir in the soft cheese and remove the pan from the heat. Use a draining spoon to place some vegetables on a pancake, then fold it into four and place it on a serving dish or individual plate. Arrange any leftover vegetables on the serving dish with the pancakes, spooning extra into the pancake cones. Pour the sauce around the pancakes and serve at once.

Bread and Bacon Supper

This is unusual, interesting and delicious.

SERVES 4

½ head Belgian endive, trimmed and broken into pieces
1 small red onion, thinly sliced and separated into rings
4 tomatoes, peeled, seeded and cut in thin wedges
½ cup olive oil
1 garlic clove, crushed
1 short French loaf, cut into chunks (or use any other crusty bread)
½ lb rindless bacon slices, roughly chopped
½ lb button mushrooms
salt and freshly ground black pepper
plenty of chopped fresh parsley
1 lemon, cut into wedges

Make a salad from the endive, onion and tomatoes, then divide it between serving plates or dishes.

Heat the oil and garlic, then stir fry the chunks of bread until they are just beginning to brown. Add the bacon to the pan and continue stir frying until the bread is part-browned and slightly crisp. The bacon should be cooked. Toss in the mushrooms, seasoning and the parsley, and stir for 2 minutes to cook the mushrooms very lightly. Divide the bread and bacon mixture between the prepared salads and add the lemon wedges for their juice.

Wheaten Eggplant

This is a hot dish inspired by the classic wheat salad known as tabbouleh.

SERVES 4

2 large eggplant, cut into cubes
salt and freshly ground black pepper
½ lb bulgar
about 3 tbsp olive oil
1 garlic clove
1 tsp dried marjoram
⅓ cup pine nuts
⅓ cup raisins
1 bunch green onions, chopped
⅓ cup chopped fresh mint
1 lemon, cut into wedges
mint sprigs to garnish

Place the eggplant in a colander and sprinkle with salt, then place over a bowl to drain for 20 minutes. Place the bulgar in a bowl and pour in enough cold water to cover it. Set aside to soak for 15 minutes.

Rinse and thoroughly drain the eggplant. Heat some olive oil and add the garlic, then stir fry the eggplant, adding more oil as needed, until they are lightly browned and tender. Add the marjoram, pine nuts and raisins, and continue stir frying the mixture for a minute or so.

Drain the bulgar and tip it into the pan, then stir it with the eggplant for a few minutes, until it is hot. Mix in the green onions and mint, and serve. Add the lemon wedges so that their juice may be squeezed over the eggplant mixture. Garnish with mint sprigs.

Saffron Shrimp with Nan

SERVES 4

2 tsp saffron strands
1 garlic clove, crushed
2 in piece fresh gingerroot, finely chopped
6 green cardamoms, slightly crushed
2 bay leaves
1 cinnamon stick, broken
⅓ cup coriander seeds, lightly crushed
1 tbsp cumin seeds
salt and black pepper
1 lb peeled cooked shrimp
4 nan bread
4 tbsp butter
1 large onion, finely chopped
¼ lb frozen peas
⅓ cup chopped fresh coriander (cilantro)
1 lemon, cut into wedges
coriander (cilantro) sprigs

Pound the saffron strands to a powder, then stir in 3 tablespoons boiling water. Mix in the garlic, ginger, cardamoms, bay leaves, cinnamon, coriander seeds, cumin and seasoning. Pour this mixture over the shrimp, scraping every last drop of saffron liquid from the container. Mix the spices with the shrimp, cover and leave to marinate for 1 hour – or longer if necessary if time permits.

Heat the nan under the broiler on a medium setting. Melt the butter and stir fry the onion for 5 minutes. Then add the shrimp and peas and stir fry for a further 5 – 7 minutes, until the spices and peas are cooked. Taste for seasoning, then pile the shrimp mixture to one side of each piece of nan. Sprinkle with coriander (cilantro) and add a lemon wedge next to the shrimp. Garnish with coriander (cilantro) leaves. Squeeze the lemon juice over the shrimp just before they are eaten.

SAFFRON PRAWNS, SERVED HERE WITH PITTA

● Couscous with Ham and Cabbage

This is an unusual way of presenting couscous, but it is quite successful.

SERVES 4

1⅓ cup couscous
¼ cup olive oil
1 large onion, halved and thinly sliced
1 lb pumpkin flesh, cut in small cubes
2 thyme sprigs
½ small green cabbage, finely shredded

¾ lb cooked ham, shredded
4 large tomatoes, peeled and cut into eighths
salt and freshly ground black pepper
4 tbsp butter, melted
plenty of chopped fresh parsley

Place the couscous in a heatproof dish. Pour on freshly boiling water to cover it by 1 in, cover and set aside for 15 minutes, by which time the grains will have swollen and they will be ready to serve.

Heat the oil, then stir fry the onion, pumpkin and thyme together for 6 – 8 minutes, or until the pumpkin is just tender.

Add the cabbage and continue stir frying for a few minutes, to lightly cook the cabbage. Toss in the ham and tomatoes and cook briefly to heat both ingredients. Taste and add seasoning to taste.

Pour the melted butter over the couscous and fork up the grains. Turn the couscous into a large dish or into individual bowls and pile the cabbage mixture in the middle. Sprinkle with parsley and serve at once.

STIRRING UP SOMETHING SPECIAL

Just to prove that stir frying can produce smart results, this chapter has plenty of ideas to grace any formal dinner party menu.

When planning a formal menu, balance a main dish that is cooked at the last minute by having accompaniments that are ready in advance. For example, have gratin-style vegetables, rice and pasta that can be cooked or popped in the oven just before the meal commences, so that you can focus all your attention on the stir frying rather than trying to drain or steam vegetables or fiddle with exacting side dishes. If you are cooking pasta as an accompaniment, use the fresh type that cooks in a couple of minutes or cook the dried type before serving the main course and transfer it to a serving dish. If it is very slightly undercooked and tossed in oil or butter with seasoning, it will outlast the time needed to serve majority of appetizers, covered and kept in a warm oven.

Remember that the finishing touches are all important to the appearance of the finished dish, so think about garnishes in advance and have them prepared, covered and kept cool if necessary. Lastly, when you clear the appetizer and exit from the dining area, let your guests know that you are about to create a splendid last-minute dish and warn them that they have a few minutes to wait.

Salmon Indienne

Salmon steaks may be used instead of fillet – cut out the bone, then cut the fish into chunks. For a less expensive alternative, look for tail pieces. Wild rice mixed with a little chopped fresh coriander (cilantro) is a good accompaniment to this dish. It adds both texture and flavor to complement the salmon.

SERVES 4

2 lb salmon fillet	2 green onions, chopped
10 green cardamoms	salt and freshly ground black
1 tbsp ground coriander	pepper
grated zest and juice of 1 lime	2 bay leaves
1 garlic clove, crushed	3 tbsp oil
1 in piece fresh gingerroot,	1 lb ripe tomatoes, peeled,
peeled and chopped	seeded and roughly chopped
1 green chili, seeded and	(see page 000)
chopped	lime wedges to garnish

Trim any skin and bones from the salmon. Cut the salmon into chunks and place in a bowl. Split the cardamom pods and place the small black seeds in a pestle. Crush them to a powder with a mortar, then mix in the coriander, lime zest and juice, garlic, ginger, chili and green onions. Add plenty of seasoning, then pour the spice mixture over the salmon and mix lightly to coat all the chunks without breaking them up. Tuck the bay leaves in among the chunks. Cover and leave to marinate for about 2 hours or longer, depending on the time available.

Heat the oil, then add the salmon with all the marinating juices and stir fry, taking care not to break the chunks, until the fish it just cooked. Stir in the tomatoes and heat through for 1 minute.

Arrange the fish on a serving platter, picking out the bay leaves as a garnish, and add the wedges of lime. The juice from the lime may be squeezed over the salmon just before it is eaten.

SALMON INDIENNE

GOLDEN TUNA WITH WATERCRESS

Golden Tuna with Watercress

Swordfish may also be cooked this way instead of the tuna. Serve the cooked mixture in small nests of cooked *paglia e fieno pasta* (thin green and white noodles, straw and hay – look for them in the fresh pasta refrigerator in the supermarket), adding a garnish of small watercress sprigs and halved orange slices.

SERVES 4

4 oranges	salt and freshly ground black
1 lb tuna steak, cubed	pepper
½ cup olive oil	1 yellow bell pepper, seeded and
½ cup dry white wine	cut into fine strips
⅓ cup snipped chives	4 yellow zucchini, thinly sliced
	2 bunches watercress, trimmed

Grate the zest and squeeze the juice from 1 orange, then pour this over the tuna fish. Add all but 1 tablespoon of the olive oil, the wine, chives and seasoning. Mix the fish with the flavoring ingredients and cover. Leave to marinate for 4 – 6 hours before cooking.

Peel the remaining oranges, removing all the pith. Hold each orange in turn over a bowl and cut between the membranes to remove the fruit segments. Catch all the juices and pour them over the fish.

Heat the remaining 1 tablespoon olive oil. Drain the tuna and reserve the marinade. Stir fry the fish until lightly browned, then use a slotted spoon to remove it from the pan and set aside. Stir fry the pepper and zucchini for 1 minute, then tip in all the marinade and bring to a boil. Boil rapidly for a minute or so, then replace the tuna and stir in the watercress leaves. Boil for another 30 – 60 seconds and remove from the heat. Carefully mix in the orange and serve at once.

Sizzling Butterfly Shrimp

Uncooked Mediterranean or jumbo shrimp are available frozen from good fishmongers and oriental supermarkets. Since they tend to be rather expensive, I have kept the portions small but the end result need not look mean with the right accompaniments: for example, serve a chow mein with some sliced scallops.

SERVES 4

24 uncooked large Mediterranean shrimp, shelled with tails on
cornstarch for coating
2-in piece fresh gingerroot, peeled and grated, then chopped into small pieces
1 garlic clove, crushed
1 green chili, seeded and finely chopped (optional)
2 tsp sugar
2 tsp white wine vinegar
½ tsp tomato paste

1 tbsp light soy sauce
1 tbsp dry sherry
pinch of five spice powder
1 tsp sesame oil
½ cup peanut oil

VEGETABLE GARNISH

6 green onions, cut into very fine strips
½ red bell pepper, seeded and cut into short, very fine strips
¼ cucumber, peeled and cut into short, fine strips
lemon wedges to serve

To prepare the shrimp, first remove the fine black cord that runs down the back (this may have been removed). Using a small sharp knife, take a shrimp and cut it down the back, almost through in half, then press it open. Repeat with all the shellfish. Coat them generously with cornstarch and shake off excess.

In a bowl, mix the ginger, garlic, chili, sugar, vinegar, tomato paste, soy sauce, sherry, five spice powder and sesame oil. Add the shrimp and mix well to coat them with the flavoring ingredients. They should be thoroughly tossed to ensure that they are all flavored with the paste.

Heat the groundnut oil until it is shimmering hot, then stir fry the shrimp over high heat until they are crisp and golden – this takes only a few minutes. Use a slotted spoon to transfer them to a serving plate.

Add all the vegetables for garnish to the oil remaining in the pan and stir fry for 2 minutes. Spoon them on the plate with the shrimp and add the lemon wedges. Serve the dish immediately.

Swordfish with Saffron

Any firm white fish is good cooked like this – halibut, monkfish or cod. New potatoes and spinach or a salad are suitable accompaniments.

SERVES 4

1½ lb swordfish steak, cut in chunks
⅓ cup sunflower oil plus extra for cooking
3 tbsp lemon juice
1 cup dry white wine
1 bay leaf
1 thyme sprig
salt and freshly ground black pepper
1 tsp saffron strands
⅓ cup all-purpose flour
2 leeks, thinly sliced
2 carrots, cut into matchstick strips
2 celery stalks, thinly sliced
1 cup half-and-half

Place the fish in a dish. In a jar with a tight-fitting lid, combine half the oil, the lemon juice, wine, bay leaf, thyme and seasoning. Shake the mixture until the oil is thoroughly combined, then pour it over the fish. Cover and leave to marinate for several hours.

Pound the saffron strands to a powder, then stir in 3 tablespoons boiling water. Stir until the saffron has dissolved completely and set aside.

Drain the fish, reserving the marinade, then mop the cubes on absorbent paper towels. Toss them in the flour, adding a little seasoning. Heat the remaining oil and stir fry the fish until golden brown. Use a slotted spoon to transfer the fish to a serving dish or individual plates and keep hot. Add a little extra oil and stir fry the leeks, carrots and celery over high heat for 2 – 3 minutes, until they are lightly cooked.

Arrange the vegetables alongside the fish, then pour the reserved marinade into the pan and bring to a boil. Boil hard until reduced by half, then reduce the heat and stir in the cream. Add the saffron liquid and heat gently to warm the cream. Do not boil. Spoon the sauce over or around the fish and serve at once.

Scallops with Zucchini

This makes a perfect light lunch – serve the seafood mixture on a base of cooked narrow noodles, wild rice or salad.

SERVES 4

3 tbsp olive oil
3 tbsp finely chopped onion
16 scallops, sliced
6 small zucchini, thinly sliced
salt and pepper
4 tarragon sprigs, leaves removed
4 tbsp half-and-half

Heat the oil and stir fry the onion over moderate heat for about 5 minutes, until softened. Stir fry the scallops for 2 minutes. Add the courgettes, seasoning and tarragon, and cook for a further 2 minutes. Neither the scallops nor the courgettes should be overcooked – the scallops, in particular, will toughen.

Add the cream, stir for a few seconds to heat it through without boiling, then serve at once.

COOK'S TIP

Crisp croûtons go well with the scallops and zucchini. Make them by frying small triangles of bread in a mixture of olive oil and butter until golden. Drain on absorbent paper towels, and arrange the croûtons around the edge of the scallop mixture on the dish.

SWORDFISH WITH SAFFRON

DUCK WITH PLUMS AND PORT

Duck with Plums and Port

Serve this rich stir fry with rice or pasta.

SERVES 4

3 duck breasts, skinned and thinly
   sliced across (into medallions)
½ cup port
grated zest and juice of 1 orange
1 bay leaf
1 parsley sprig
1 thyme sprig
1 rosemary sprig
¼ cup all-purpose flour

salt and freshly ground black
   pepper
3 tbsp oil
knob of butter
½ lb plums, halved, pitted and
   quartered

GARNISH (OPTIONAL)
orange slices
fresh herbs

Place the duck in a dish. Add the port, orange zest and juice, and all the herbs. Mix well, cover and leave to marinate overnight.

Strain the duck well, reserving the marinade. Pick out the herbs, then pat the duck on absorbent paper towels. Toss the slices of duck in the flour, adding plenty of seasoning.

Heat the oil and butter with the herbs. Add the duck and stir fry the pieces until lightly browned. Sprinkle any leftover flour into the pan, then stir in the marinade and add the plums. Stir all the time until the juices boil and thicken. Reduce the heat and cook for 2 minutes, then taste for seasoning before serving. Halved orange slices and fresh herbs may be added for garnish.

Flambé Chicken with Peaches

Dried peaches give this dish a wonderfully rich, fruity flavor. Rice, pasta and plain, boiled baby potatoes are all suitable accompaniments; however, for a lighter meal, the cooked chicken may be served on a crisp salad of mixed leaves, with warm fresh bread.

SERVES 4
1 cup dried peaches
1 tbsp oil
knob of butter
2 rosemary sprigs
strip of lemon zest
4 boneless chicken breasts,
   skinned and cubed

salt and freshly ground black
   pepper
⅓ cup brandy

GARNISH
1 fresh peach, pitted and sliced
rosemary sprigs

Place the peaches in a small basin, then pour in just enough cold water to cover them. Cover and leave to soak overnight.

Drain the peaches, reserving the liquid, then cut them into small pieces. Heat the oil and butter, then add the rosemary and lemon zest. Stir fry these aromatics for about 30 seconds before adding the chicken – this gives the cooking fat a good flavor. Sprinkle in seasoning, then stir fry the chicken until the pieces are golden and cooked through.

Pour in the peaches and their soaking liquid, bring to a boil and stir over medium to high heat until most of the liquid has evaporated and the chicken is well glazed and juicy. Transfer the chicken to a serving dish, discarding the lemon zest and cooked rosemary. Garnish the chicken with peach slices and rosemary.

Add the brandy to the pan (it will still be hot enough to warm the brandy without requiring any further heating) and swirl it around before pouring over the chicken and igniting it. Take the flaming chicken to the table and serve it as soon as the flames have subsided.

COOK'S TIP

To prevent cut peaches from turning brown, dip the pieces in lemon juice and keep them covered until they are used.

Glazed Lamb

The fillet of lamb is the eye of meat cut from the best end or middle neck. Sliced into neat rounds, as here, the portions are referred to as medallions. A border of piped mashed potatoes or small baby potatoes will complement the rich, honey glaze which coats the stir fried lamb with plums.

SERVES 4

2 lb lamb fillet, sliced into neat circles
4 rosemary sprigs
3 tbsp clear honey
1 cup medium cider
¼ cup all-purpose flour
salt and freshly ground black pepper
3 tbsp peanut oil
1 small onion, finely chopped
½ lb red plums, halved and pitted
rosemary sprigs to garnish

Place the meat in a dish and add the rosemary, honey and cider. Mix well, cover and leave to marinate for several hours or overnight.

Drain the meat well, reserving all the marinade. Then sprinkle the flour and plenty of seasoning over the pieces of lamb.

Heat the oil and stir fry the onion for 3 – 4 minutes. Add the lamb and stir fry until browned all over. Pour in the marinade and add the plums. Boil quite hard for about 2 minutes, so that the marinade reduces and the plums cook. Stir to prevent the meat sticking to the pan. When the meat and plums are well glazed in sauce, transfer them to a serving dish. Add some rosemary sprigs as a garnish.

Minted Lamb with Lentils

SERVES 4

½ lb green lentils
1 lb lean boneless lamb diced
1 garlic clove (optional)
3 tbsp chopped fresh mint
salt and freshly ground pepper
3 tbsp olive oil

1 onion, chopped
½ lb mushrooms, sliced
dash of Worcestershire sauce
1 lb tomatoes, peeled and roughly
   chopped
1 cup Greek-style yogurt
mint sprigs to garnish (optional)

Cook the lentils in plenty of boiling water for 35 minutes or until tender, but not mushy. Drain well and set aside.

Thoroughly mix the lamb with the garlic (if used), mint and plenty of seasoning. Heat the oil and stir fry the onion for 5 minutes before adding the lamb. Continue stir frying until the meat is cooked and well-browned. Stir in the mushrooms and Worcestershire sauce and stir fry for a further 5 minutes.

Tip the lentils into the lamb mixture and stir in the tomatoes. Stir fry for another 3 – 5 minutes so that the lentils and tomatoes are hot. Taste for seasoning, then divide between individual serving dishes and top each portion with a little yoghurt. Garnish with mint sprigs, if liked, and serve the remaining yoghurt separately.

Oriental Ginger Lamb

A small, local, undistinguished Chinese restaurant includes a number of special dishes on its menu and this is based on one of them – it's very simple, absolutely bursting with flavor and ideal for fellow ginger fans! It is a dish to make when you can buy juicy, young ginger, which is plump and thin skinned – look out for it in Chinese supermarkets. Remember to warn unsuspecting guests that there are whole ginger slices in among the pieces of meat – when the ginger is young and tender, the slices are, of course, perfectly edible, but many people prefer to avoid them.

SERVES 4

1 lb lean boneless lamb, cut into
   small, thin slices
2-in piece, young fresh
   gingerroot, peeled and very
   thinly sliced
⅓ cup soy sauce
⅓ cup dry sherry
1 tsp sugar

1 tbsp lemon juice
1 tbsp cornstarch
1 cup lamb or chicken broth
¼ cup oil
1 tsp sesame oil
1 garlic clove
1 bunch green onions, cut in 1-in
   lengths

Place the lamb in a dish and mix in the ginger. Stir the soy sauce, sherry, sugar and lemon juice together, then pour the mixture over the lamb and ginger. Cover and leave to marinate for several hours.

Blend the cornstarch to a smooth paste with a little of the broth, then stir in the remaining broth. Heat the oil and sesame oil, add the garlic and use a slotted spoon to add the lamb and ginger to the pan. Stir fry the lamb until browned, then add the green onions and continue stir frying for 2 minutes.

Pour in the marinating juices from the lamb and the stock. Bring to a boil and simmer, stirring, for 5 minutes. Taste for seasoning before serving, adding a little extra soy sauce if necessary.

ORIENTAL GINGER LAMB

BEEF IN OYSTER SAUCE

Beef in Oyster Sauce

Include this as part of a Chinese menu, in which case the quantities may be reduced by half, or serve it with plain cooked rice or chow mein.

SERVES 4

1 lb frying steak, cut into small, thin slices	4 large dried Chinese mushrooms
¼ cup oyster sauce	⅓ cup oil
3 tbsp soy sauce	1 green bell pepper, seeded and cut into chunks
1 garlic clove, crushed	1 red bell pepper, seeded and cut into chunks
⅓ cup dry sherry	1 onion, cut into chunks

Place the meat in a dish. Mix the oyster sauce, soy sauce, garlic and sherry together, then pour the mixture over the meat and mix well. Cover and leave to marinate for 2 – 4 hours. Place the mushrooms in a small basin or mug and pour in just enough hot water to cover them. Place a saucer or the base of another mug on the mushrooms to keep them submerged, then leave to soak for 20 minutes. Drain, reserving the soaking liquid, discard tough stalks and slice the mushroom caps.

Heat the oil, then stir fry the peppers and onion for 3 minutes. Use a draining spoon to add the beef to the pan, then continue stir frying until the meat is cooked and lightly browned. Add the mushrooms.

Pour the soaking liquid into the oyster sauce marinade left from the meat and mix well, then pour the liquid into the pan. Bring to a boil and boil rapidly for a few minutes so that the meat is coated in a slightly thickened sauce. Serve at once.

Beef Stroganoff

This classic dish of quick-fried steak with sour cream takes its name from the Russian Count Stroganoff. The colds of northern Siberia rendered the Count's beef virtually frozen, such that it could only be cut into the thinnest slices. Plain cooked rice and a good, very crisp, fresh mixed green salad will make the meal a real treat.

SERVES 4

2 lb good beef steak (at least rump or topside, fillet if you are feeling extravagent)	large knob of butter
	1 onion, halved and thinly sliced
	½ lb mushrooms, thinly sliced
salt and freshly ground black pepper	⅓ cup brandy
	⅔ cup sour cream
½ tsp paprika	plenty of chopped fresh parsley
3 tbsp olive oil	

Place the meat in the freezer until it is icy and very firm. Use a sharp knife to cut the beef across the grain into the thinnest slices possible, then cut them across into strips. Season the beef and sprinkle with paprika.

Heat the oil and butter, then stir fry the onion for 5 minutes. Add the mushrooms and stir fry for a further 3 minutes, taking care not to break up the mushroom slices. Push the onion and mushrooms to one side of the pan, then stir fry the meat over high heat until all the strips are browned.

Sprinkle in the brandy and mix the meat with the onion and mushrooms. Pour in the sour cream and heat briefly without allowing it to boil. Quickly toss in plenty of parsley and serve at once.

BEEF STROGANOFF

Marinated Venison with Red Cabbage

Small baked potatoes in their skins or cooked buckwheat (see Pork with Orange), mixed with plenty of chopped parsley, go well with this venison dish.

SERVES 4

1 lb venison steak (suitable for frying), trimmed of all fat and cut in strips
1 cup red wine
1 blade of mace
1 bay leaf
6 juniper berries, crushed
salt and freshly ground black pepper
¼ cup all-purpose flour
⅓ cup olive oil
1 large onion, halved and thinly sliced
1 lb red cabbage, finely shredded
¼ cup soft brown sugar
3 tbsp cider vinegar

Place the venison in a dish, then add the wine, mace, bay leaf, juniper and plenty of seasoning. Mix well, cover and marinate for 24 hours.

Drain the meat, reserving the marinade. Pat the meat dry on absorbent paper towels, then toss it with the flour until it is well mixed.

Heat half the oil and stir fry the onion for 5 minutes. Add the venison and stir fry for about 10 minutes, or until the strips are well browned. Use a slotted spoon to remove the meat from the pan.

Add the remaining oil and stir fry the cabbage for 5 – 7 minutes, or until it is slightly softened. Sprinkle in the sugar and vinegar and add a little seasoning, then stir fry for a further 2 minutes. Replace the meat and mix well, then pour in the reserved marinade. Bring to a boil and simmer for 5 minutes. Discard the blade of mace before serving the venison.

Steak with Anchovies and Olives

Pasta or a classic, creamy risotto are ideal accompaniments for this Italian-style steak stir fry.

SERVES 4

1½ lb frying steak, cut into strips
1 garlic clove, crushed
3 tbsp tomato paste
1 cup red wine
salt and freshly ground black pepper
⅓ cup all-purpose flour
⅓ cup olive oil
1 onion, halved and thinly sliced
1 green bell pepper, halved, seeded and thinly sliced
2-oz can anchovy fillets, drained and chopped
1 cup black olives, pitted and sliced
3 tbsp chopped parsley
handful of basil leaves, coarsely shredded

Place the steak in a dish. Mix the garlic, tomato paste and red wine with seasoning, then pour the mixture over the steak. Mix well, cover and leave the meat to marinate overnight.

Drain the steak, reserving the marinade. Pat the strips of meat dry on absorbent paper towels, then toss them in the flour.

EAK WITH ANCHOVIES AND OLIVES

Heat ¼ cup of the olive oil, then stir fry the onion and bell pepper for 5 minutes. Add the steak and stir fry over fairly high heat until the strips are evenly browned. Pour in the reserved marinade and stir until the sauce boils. Simmer for 5 minutes, stirring, then taste for seasoning before transferring the meat mixture to a serving dish.

Wipe out the pan and heat the remaining olive oil. Add the anchovies, olives and parsley and toss them in the hot oil for 30 seconds. Stir in the basil, then pour the mixture over the steak and serve at once.

DESALTING ANCHOVIES

For a milder less salty result, the anchovy fillets may be drained, soaked in a little milk for 5 minutes, then drained again.

● Pork with Pernod

If you do not have any Pernod, then substitute Greek ouzo or Turkish raki. Rice or couscous will complement the full flavor of this simple dish.

SERVES 4

1½ lb lean boneless pork, diced
2 sage sprigs
2 thyme sprigs
½ cup Pernod or other aniseed
   liquor
salt and freshly ground black
   pepper
3 tbsp olive oil
1 leek, thinly sliced

2 small carrots, diced
½ lb button mushrooms, sliced
1 cup sour cream
8 large Iceberg lettuce leaves
tarragon sprigs to garnish
   (optional)

Place the pork in a dish with the sage and thyme, then pour in the Pernod or other liquor. Add some seasoning, mix well and cover. Leave to marinate for about 2 hours.

Heat the oil, then stir fry the leek and carrots for 5 minutes. Use a draining spoon to add the pork to the pan, with the herb sprigs. Reserve the marinade. Stir fry the pork until lightly browned, then add the mushrooms and stir fry for a further 2 – 3 minutes before pouring in the marinade.

Bring the juices to a boil, reduce the heat and pour in the sour cream. Heat for 1 minute but do not allow the cream to boil. Taste for seasoning.

Arrange the lettuce leaves on a serving platter and spoon the pork mixture into them. Garnish with tarragon, if liked, and serve at once.

● Turkey Nests

You need to have two fine metal strainers or a special frying basket to make the nests in which to serve this stir fry. If you do not want to go to all the trouble of making the nests, the stir fry may also be served in crispy baked potato shells, pastry shells – as in Turkey and Broccoli Tartlets – or pancakes.

SERVES 4

6–8 oz Chinese egg noodles (see Cook's Tip)
oil for deep frying
¼ lb cream cheese
3 tbsp chopped fresh parsley
1 tsp chopped fresh thyme
1 tsp grated lemon zest
3 tbsp olive oil
1 lb boneless turkey breast, finely shredded

1 red bell pepper, seeded and finely shredded
salt and freshly ground black pepper
¼ lb fine green beans, blanched in boiling water for 1 minute
¼ lb lean cooked ham, shredded

Add the noodles to boiling water and bring back to a boil. Drain and rinse under cold water. Drain well.

Thoroughly grease two metal strainers: one measuring about 1 in larger than the other. The larger strainer should be about 4 in in diameter – no bigger. Heat the oil for deep frying. Line the larger strainer with a layer of noodles and press the smaller one inside to hold the noodles in place. Deep fry the noodles until golden, then remove them from the strainer and leave to drain on absorbent paper towels. Make eight nests. The nests can be made in advance and reheated in a very hot oven for a few minutes before serving – they must be crisp.

Mix the cream cheese, parsley, thyme and lemon zest, then shape into eight small pats and chill them.

Heat the oil, then stir fry the turkey and pepper, adding seasoning, until the turkey is lightly browned and the pepper tender. Stir in the beans and continue cooking for 3 minutes to heat them through. Lastly, add the ham and cook for a minute or so.

Divide the stir-fried mixture between the nests and top each with a pat of flavored cream cheese.

COOK'S TIP

About ¼ lb noodles will make 5 nests; therefore ½ lb will make 10 nests; this allows for breakages.

● Turkey and Broccoli Tartlets

The tartlets may be made well ahead and heated through gently just before serving.

SERVES 4

2 cups all-purpose flour
¾ cup butter
⅓ cup cranberry sauce
3 tbsp sunflower oil
½ lb boneless turkey breast, cut into fine strips

salt and freshly ground black pepper
¼ lb broccoli flowerets, broken into small pieces
½ cup walnuts, chopped
2 green onions, chopped
⅓ cup heavy cream
a little chopped fresh parsley

Set the oven at 400°F. Place the flour in a bowl and rub in the butter, then mix in just enough water to bind the ingredients into a dough. Roll out and use it to line four individual, loose-bottomed tart tin. Prick the base of the pastry all over, then chill the cases for 30 minutes.

Place a piece of waxed paper and some dried peas or baking beans in each tartlet, and bake for 20 minutes. Remove the beans and paper and cook for a further 5 – 10 minutes, or until the pastry is golden.

Spread a little cranberry sauce in each tartlet. Heat the oil and stir fry the turkey, adding seasoning, until lightly browned. Stir in the broccoli, walnuts and green onions and continue stir frying for a further 3 – 5 minutes, until the broccoli is bright and slightly tender.

Fill the tartlets with the turkey mixture and spoon a little cream over each one. Sprinkle with parsley.

● Veal with Vermouth

A bowl of buttered noodles and a salad will taste good with this simple veal dish.

SERVES 4

4 veal escalopes, beaten out thinly, then cut into strips
¼ cup all-purpose flour
salt and freshly ground black pepper
3 tbsp oil
knob of butter
¼ lb rindless smoked bacon slices, diced
1 small onion, thinly sliced

1 cup dry white vermouth
15-oz can artichoke hearts, drained
⅓ cup heavy cream
1 cup black grapes, halved and deseeded (if necessary)

GARNISH (OPTIONAL)
4 small sprigs of grapes
fresh herbs

Toss the veal with the flour and seasoning. Heat the oil and butter, then stir fry the bacon and onion for 5 minutes. Add the veal and continue to stir fry until the strips of meat are lightly browned.

Pour in the vermouth and bring to a boil, stirring all the time. Add the artichoke hearts and simmer for 3 minutes. Stir in the cream and grapes, then transfer the cooked veal to a serving dish or individual plates. Garnish with grapes and fresh herbs, if liked.

AS AN ASIDE

Stir fried accompaniments can pep up long-cooked main dishes adding contrasting color, texture and a fresh, zingy flavor. Consider these recipes too, when you plan a barbecue or buffet-style lunch, stirring them up at the last minute to refresh plain or cold centerpieces.

The dishes include satisfying rice, grains and bean ensembles, as well as light vegetable mixtures. If you are looking for an interesting, simple supper dish, you may even find the right candidate here by serving simple vegetable combinations as a topping for fresh cooked pasta.

Use the information in the recipes to create very simple side dishes, combining one or two vegetables with some herbs or seasoning. Let the flavor of the fresh ingredients dominate the dish and you will not be far away from perfect results.

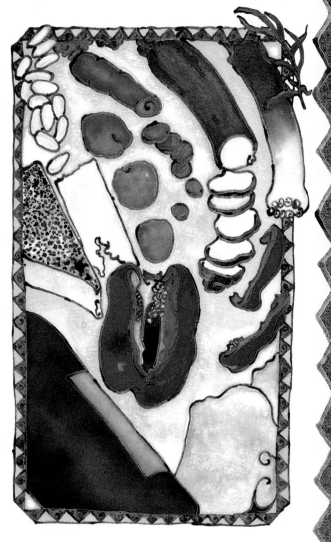

Summer Vegetables

This refreshing mixture of yellow vegetables is interesting enough to transform plain, cooked pasta into a complete meal. It also turns plain, broiled fish, poultry or meat into a splendid main course.

SERVES 4

½ lb baby corn cobs
¼ cup olive oil
1 yellow bell pepper, seeded and thinly sliced
1 small onion, halved and thinly sliced
4 yellow zucchini, thinly sliced

6 yellow tomatoes, halved, seeded and cut in thin strips
salt and freshly ground black pepper
handful of basil leaves
1 tbsp grated lemon zest
¼ cup chopped fresh parsley
1 small garlic clove, finely chopped (optional)

Cover the corn cobs with water and bring them to a boil. Continue to boil for 2 minutes, then drain the corn and set aside.

Heat the oil, then stir fry the pepper and onion for 5 – 8 minutes, until softened. Add the corn and continue to stir fry for another 5 minutes or until the corn and onion are cooked, but still slightly crunchy.

Toss in the zucchini and tomatoes and stir fry for about 3 minutes – just long enough to heat the vegetables and take the raw edge off the zucchini. Sprinkle in seasoning to taste and the basil leaves, and mix well. Turn the vegetables into a serving dish or individual side plates. Mix the lemon zest, parsley and garlic, if liked, then sprinkle this mixture over the vegetables. Serve at once.

Winter Stir Fry

This tasty root vegetable mixture goes well with simple foods like poached or fried eggs, broiled bacon or other broiled meats.

SERVES 4

2 large potatoes, coarsely grated
2 large carrots, coarsely grated
1 parsnip, coarsely grated
3 tbsp all-purpose flour
salt and pepper

⅓ cup oil
1 large onion, chopped
½ lb white cabbage, finely shredded

Rinse the potatoes under plenty of cold water, then drain them and squeeze out excess moisture so that the shreds separate. Mix the potatoes with the carrots and parsnip. Sprinkle in the flour and plenty of seasoning, then toss the vegetable shreds with the flour using a fork.

Heat the oil and stir fry the onion for 3 minutes. Add the grated vegetables and stir fry for about 15 minutes, or until they are lightly browned. As the vegetables are cooking they should be turned over and mixed from the center outwards, and from the sides of the pan to the middle, so that the shreds brown and stay separate. If the vegetables are stirred in a circular direction they will brown underneath, and they tend to stick together in a large clump.

Add the cabbage and continue to stir fry for another 5 – 7 minutes, or until the cabbage is lightly cooked and the other vegetables are browned. Serve at once.

WINTER STIR FRY

● Rice with Spinach

SERVES 4

¾ cup long-grain rice, cooked
¼ cup oil
½ small onion, chopped
3 tbsp cumin seeds

1 tsp turmeric
knob of butter (optional)
½ lb fresh spinach, cooked,
   drained and shredded

The rice should be freshly cooked and drained if necessary. If cooked by the absorption method, do not fork up the grains but leave the pan covered off the heat when the rice is cooked.

Heat the oil and stir fry the onion with the cumin seeds for 5 minutes. Stir in the turmeric and continue to cook for 2 minutes before adding the butter, if used. Allow the butter to melt, then add the rice and stir fry for 2 minutes until it has become well coated in the flavoring ingredients.

Make a well in the rice or push it to one side of the pan and add the spinach. Stir fry the spinach briefly to heat it through. Then fork the spinach into the rice and serve at once.

● Cucumber with Ham

Another quick stir fry to serve as a side dish or with some rice or pasta, or in a baked potato as a light main course. This is delicious with poached or broiled chicken or turkey.

SERVES 4

1 cucumber, peeled, halved
   lengthwise and sliced
   (about 1 lb)
salt and freshly ground black
   pepper

½ lb lean cooked ham, cut into
   small cubes
3 green onions, chopped
3 tsp paprika
2 tbsp oil
1 garlic clove, crushed (optional)

The cucumber slices should be about ⅛ in thick. Place them in a colander or strainer, and sprinkle with a little salt, then leave over a bowl to drain for 15 minutes. Pat all the slices dry on absorbent paper towels.

Place the ham in a bowl with the green onions. Add the paprika and a little freshly ground black pepper, then mix well to coat the ham in the seasoning.

Heat the oil, then stir fry the garlic, if used, and ham for 5 minutes to lightly brown the meat and seal on the seasoning. Add the cucumber and continue stir frying for another 5 minutes, to lightly cook the vegetable. Serve at once.

RICE WITH SPINACH

SLIGHTLY SPICY LEEKS

Slightly Spicy Leeks

I like the combination of orange, leek and spice –
particularly with broiled or barbecued mackerel, duck,
sausages, gammon or pork. However, if the orange
clashes with your main dish it may be omitted or the
zest of half a lemon may be added instead.

SERVES 4

⅓ cup oil
3 tbsp crushed coriander seeds
grated zest and juice of 1 orange
¼ tsp ground allspice

1 lb leeks, thinly sliced and
  separated into rings
salt and freshly ground black
  pepper

Heat the oil, then stir fry the crushed coriander with the
orange rind and allspice over fairly low heat for 2 – 3
minutes, or until the orange rind is quite bright and the
mixture is fragrant.

Toss in all the leeks and increase the heat, then stir
fry the vegetables for about 8 minutes, or until they are
softened. Add the orange juice and boil hard for 2
minutes, tossing the leeks to coat them in a spicy glaze.
Taste and add seasoning, then serve at once.

Celeriac with Peas

Celeriac is a swede-like vegetable with thick, pale skin
and a crunchy texture. It has a mild celery flavour and is
excellent eaten raw or cooked, making it an ideal stir fry
candidate.

SERVES 6

1 small to medium celeriac root,
  peeled and cut in short thin
  strips
juice of ½ lemon
3 tbsp olive oil

1 small leek, cut in short strips
½ lb shelled peas, frozen or
  blanched fresh
a little freshly grated nutmeg
salt and freshly ground black
  pepper

Cut the celeriac into pieces, placing it in a bowl of cold
water with the lemon juice added to prevent it
discoloring.

Heat the oil and stir fry the leek for about 3 minutes.
Drain the celeriac, shake off the water and add it to the
leek. Stir fry fairly vigorously for 5 minutes, then add the
peas and continue to stir fry for another 5 minutes. The
peas should be just cooked and the celeriac should still
be crisp. Add a little nutmeg and seasoning to taste
before serving the vegetables.

RICE AND BEANS

🔵 Rice and Beans

SERVES 4 – 6

3 tbsp oil
1 large onion, chopped
2 celery stalks, thinly sliced
1 garlic clove, crushed
3 tbsp sunflower seeds
3 tbsp sesame seeds
2 × 15-oz cans red kidney beans, drained

2 tsp dried marjoram
salt and freshly ground black pepper
¾ cup long-grain brown or white rice, freshly cooked
⅓ cup chopped parsley

Heat the oil, then stir fry the onion, celery and garlic for 10 – 15 minutes until the onion is softened, but not browned. Stir in the seeds and continue to cook for 2 minutes. Add the beans, marjoram and seasoning, and stir fry for a further 2 – 3 minutes to heat them through.

Tip in the rice and stir fry it for a few minutes to combine the ingredients and allow the flavors to mingle. Fork in the parsley and serve at once.

COOK'S TIP

This is a good way of using up leftover cooked rice. However, remember that the rice should be thoroughly heated before serving, therefore it should be stir fried for longer.

🔵 Piquant Green Beans

If using frozen beans for this stir fry, there is no need to blanch them before frying. If fresh dill is not available, don't bother with dried dill weed – it is better to use fresh parsley instead.

SERVES 4

1 lb fine French beans, trimmed
1 tbsp olive oil
1 tbsp sunflower oil
½ small onion, finely chopped
1 dill pickle, diced

1 tbsp capers, chopped
salt and freshly ground black pepper
2 eggs, hard-boiled and chopped
3 tbsp chopped fresh dill

Plunge the beans into boiling water, bring the water back to a boil, then drain the beans. Heat both oils, then stir fry the onion and cucumber for about 3 minutes, until the onion is slightly softened.

Stir in the beans, capers and seasoning. Continue to stir fry for a further 3 minutes or until the beans are hot and cooked, but still crunchy. Transfer to a serving dish or individual plates and sprinkle with the egg and dill. Serve at once.

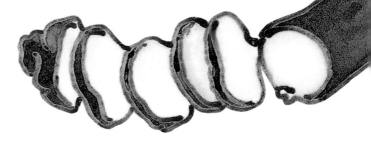

Spinach with Apples and Walnuts

SERVES 4

1 lb fresh spinach
¼ cup olive oil
½ small onion, finely chopped
2 full-flavored eating apples,
   peeled, cored and diced

scant cup walnut pieces, chopped
knob of butter (optional)
salt and freshly ground black
   pepper

Wash the spinach, then place it dripping wet in a large pan. Cover with a lid and cook over high heat, shaking the pan often, for about 3 minutes, or until the spinach has reduced in volume and softened. Drain well, pressing all the liquid from the spinach.

Heat the oil, then stir fry the onion and apples until the onion has softened, but not browned. Stir in the nuts and continue stir frying for about 5 minutes to roast them and bring out their flavor. Add the butter and heat it through before adding the spinach. Stir fry the spinach for 3 minutes. Add seasoning to taste and then serve at once.

Carrots with Caraway

This may be made using old carrots, in which case they should be cut into small sticks (they do not have to be as fine as julienne) or into even slices. If caraway is not your favorite spice, try substituting fennel seeds instead – they are also good with carrots and orange.

SERVES 4 – 6

1 lb whole baby carrots
3 tbsp olive oil
1 small onion, finely chopped

1 tbsp caraway seeds
knob of butter (optional)
juice of 1 large orange

Plunge the carrots into just enough boiling water to cover them and bring the water back to a boil. Boil for 2 minutes, then drain the carrots.

Heat the oil and stir fry the onion with the caraway seeds until the onion is softened, but not browned. Add the butter, if used, and allow it to melt. Tip the carrots into the pan and stir fry them for 3 minutes before adding the orange juice.

Boil the orange juice rapidly, turning the carrots all the time, until it is reduced to a slightly caramelized glaze which coats the vegetables. The carrots should be crunchy but not hard, and they should be coated in a full-flavored glaze. Serve at once.

SPINACH WITH APPLES AND WALNUTS

Chop Suey

Use this as a basis for a variety of dishes – stir fry shredded raw chicken breast, pork or beef before adding the vegetables to make a main course dish. Alternatively, add some peeled cooked shrimp (thawed if frozen) with the bean spouts. Also, the combination of vegetables may be changed to suit the season or the contents of the salad drawer in the refrigerator – remember, however, that bean sprouts are the essential ingredient for a chop suey.

SERVES 4

2 tsp cornstarch	1 celery stalk, cut into fine short
3 tbsp soy sauce	strips
1 tbsp dry sherry	1 green bell pepper, seeded and
3 tbsp oil	cut into fine short strips
1 tsp sesame oil	½ onion, thinly sliced
	12 oz bean sprouts

Blend the cornstarch with the soy sauce, sherry and 3 tablespoons of water; set aside.

Heat both oils together, then stir fry the celery, pepper and onion for 5 minutes. The vegetables should be lightly cooked and still crunchy. Toss in the bean sprouts and stir fry for 1 minute. Give the cornstarch mixture a stir, pour it into the pan and bring the juices to a boil, stirring all the time. Cook for 2 minutes, stirring, then serve at once.

CHOP SUEY

PUMPKIN WITH LEEKS

Pumpkin with Leeks

I find that stir frying is one of the best cooking methods for pumpkin – the vegetable remains whole but slightly tender. Turn this into a tasty supper dish by stir frying some diced, rindless bacon with the leeks.

SERVES 4

3 tbsp oil	⅓ cup white raisins
knob of butter	1 lb prepared pumpkin flesh,
1 garlic clove, crushed (optional)	cubed
2 leeks, sliced	salt and freshly ground black
2 tsp ground cinnamon	pepper

Heat the oil and butter until the butter melts, then add the garlic (if wished), leeks, cinnamon and white raisins. Stir fry the leeks for 5 minutes until they are softened.

Add the pumpkin and seasoning. Continue stir frying until the cubes are tender, but not soft enough to become mushy, which takes about 7 – 10 minutes. Serve the dish at once.

Beets with Horseradish

SERVES 4

⅓ cup oil
2 onions, halved and thinly sliced
1 lb cooked beets, cut in small
  cubes
salt and freshly ground black
  pepper
¼ cup chopped fresh dill
⅓ cup horseradish sauce
½ cup sour cream

Heat the oil and stir fry the onions for 10 minutes, until they are quite well cooked and beginning to brown. Add the beets with seasoning and continue to stir fry for about 5 minutes for the beets to become hot, and for the flavor of the onions to mingle with it. Stir in the dill and transfer the beets to a serving dish.

Mix the horseradish sauce with the sour cream and trickle this over the beets. Serve at once, tossing the horseradish cream with the beets and onion as the vegetables are spooned out.

CORIANDER POTATOES

Coriander Potatoes

Coriander is one of my favorite spices – it works wonders for new potatoes, complementing their sweet fresh flavor perfectly.

SERVES 4

2 lb baby potatoes, scrubbed and boiled	3 tbsp lemon juice
	⅓ cup olive oil
salt and freshly ground black pepper	¼ cup crushed coriander seeds
	strip of lemon zest
2 tsp superfine sugar	⅓ cup snipped chives

Cook the potatoes in boiling, slightly salted water for 10 – 15 minutes, or until tender. Drain. Stir the sugar and lemon juice together until the sugar dissolves.

Heat the oil and stir fry the coriander for 2 minutes. Add the lemon zest and continue to cook for a further minute, pressing the piece of zest to bring out its flavor. Tip the potatoes into the pan and then stir fry them for about 10 minutes, or until they are just beginning to brown on the outside.

Pour the sweetened lemon juice over the potatoes and mix them well with the oil in the pan, so that the liquids mingle to form a hot dressing. Mix in the chives, check the seasoning and serve at once.

Cracked Wheat with Zucchini

Do not confuse cracked wheat with bulgar – cracked wheat is broken not cooked.

SERVES 4

¾ cup cracked wheat	¼ cup slivered almonds
⅓ cup olive oil	½ lb small zucchini, thinly sliced
strip of lemon zest	salt and black pepper
1 bay leaf	plenty of chopped fresh parsley
2 rosemary sprigs	lemon wedges to serve
1 onion, finely chopped	(optional)

Heat the oil, then stir fry the lemon zest, bay leaf, rosemary and onion for about 10 minutes, or until the onion is softened and the herbs release their flavor. Add the slivered almonds after 5 minutes so that they are lightly browned at the end of this stage.

Next add the zucchini and stir fry them for about 2 minutes, so that they are very lightly cooked – this way their flavor will be at its best. Sprinkle in seasoning, then tip the cracked wheat into the pan. Stir well for a minute or so to mix the ingredients.

Add plenty of chopped parsley and remove the herb sprigs if you prefer before serving, or pick out the herbs to garnish the top of the wheat mixture. Lemon wedges may be served so that their juice can be squeezed over the zucchini and wheat just before eating.

Put the wheat into a strainer, and rinse it well under cold, running water. Place the grain in a pan with plenty of cold water. Bring to a boil and reduce the heat so that the water simmers. Cook the wheat for 20 minutes until tender. Drain and set aside.

Cauliflower and Celery Stir Fry

SERVES 4–6

¼ cup oil
1 small onion, halved and thinly
   sliced
½ small cauliflower, broken into
   small flowerets
1 celery heart, thinly sliced
salt and freshly ground black
   pepper

½ cup stoned black olives, sliced
1 sweet eating apple, cored and
   roughly chopped
1 tbsp capers, chopped
1 tbsp raw brown sugar
2 – 3 tbsp cider vinegar

Heat the oil and stir fry the onion for 5 minutes before
adding the cauliflower and celery. Stir fry the vegetables
until they are lightly cooked – they should not taste raw
but should still be crunchy. This takes about 15 minutes,
depending on the heat and the size of the pan.

   Add seasoning, the olives, apple, capers, and continue
to stir fry for 2 minutes. Make a well in the middle of the
vegetables and add the sugar and 2 tablespoons of the
vinegar. Stir the juices until the sugar dissolves, then
toss the small amount of dressing with the vegetables.
Taste and add the remaining vinegar if liked. Serve at
once.

Broccoli with Avocado

SERVES 4

1 lb young broccoli spears, cut in
   small pieces
2 avocados, halved, pitted, peeled
   and diced
juice of ½ lemon

¼ cup olive oil
2 green onions, chopped
salt and freshly ground black
   pepper
a few basil sprigs, leaves removed

Trim any long stalks from the broccoli and chop these to
insure that all the vegetable is evenly cooked. Toss the
avocados in the lemon juice to prevent discoloration.

   Heat the oil, then stir fry the broccoli and green
onions for about 5 minutes, or until cooked but still firm.
Add seasoning and the avocados, then stir fry for
another minute or so to heat the avocado. Toss in the
basil leaves and serve at once.

CAULIFLOWER AND CELERY STIR FRY

STIRRING SWEETS

The idea of stir frying a dessert may seem a little bizarre and I have to admit that it is a bit of a gimmick; however, these stir fries are all recipes that would excite gastric juices rather than raise eyebrows if they went by a cooking method of any other name.

Based mainly on fruit, the combinations of flavorings and serving ideas certainly do not stretch stir frying beyond sensible limits. Since fruit reacts with uncoated metal, a carbon steel wok is not the ideal cooking pan for many of these recipes – better to use a large skillet. Do not shy away from making this the second stir fry of the meal – as long as your choice of ingredients is balanced, the method is unlikely to dominate and cause a clash. Do remember to have a clean pan ready though. Since many fruits discolor if they are cut and exposed to air for any length of time, sprinkle prepared ingredients with a little lemon juice and cover closely if you are preparing them in advance.

PEARS WITH CASSIS

Pears with Cassis

SERVES 4

8 small, firm pears, peeled, cored
   and quartered
juice of 1 large orange
knob of unsalted butter
½ cup cassis (blackcurrant
   liqueur)

⅓ cup flaked almonds, toasted
sprigs of blackcurrants or halved
   orange slices to decorate
whipped cream to serve

Toss the pears in the orange juice. Melt the butter, then
add the pears, reserving the juice, and stir fry until they
are softened but still retaining their shape.

   Pour the orange juice and cassis over the pears and
mix well to coat all the pieces of fruit in sauce. Transfer
to four dishes and sprinkle each portion with flaked
almonds. Decorate with blackcurrant sprigs or halved
orange slices when blackcurrants are not available.
Serve at once, with whipped cream.

Maple Fruits

The pears should be quite firm, but not hard and
crunchy in texture.

SERVES 4

4 firm pears, peeled, cored and
   thickly sliced lengthwise
2 firm, ripe peaches, peeled,
   pitted and thickly sliced

juice of 1 lemon
4 tbsp unsalted butter
½ lb strawberries
½ cup maple syrup

Toss the pears and peaches in lemon juice as they are
prepared, keeping them separate. Melt the butter and
stir fry the pears over a fairly high heat until they are
lightly browned around the edges.

   Add the peach slices and continue stir frying for a
minute or so to heat them through. Stir in the
strawberries, any remaining lemon juice and the maple
syrup. Stir the fruit briefly to coat all the pieces in syrup.
Divide the fruits between four dishes and serve at once.

COOK'S TIP

To peel peaches, place them in a flameproof bowl
and pour freshly boiling water over to cover the
fruit. Leave to stand for about 1 minute: firm fruit
may need 1½ – 2 minutes to loosen the skin whereas
ripe fruit may be ready after 45 seconds. If the fruit
is allowed to stand too long it will begin to cook and
become soft.

   Drain the peaches and slit the skin with the point
of a knife, then it should peel off easily. Remember
to toss cut or peeled peaches in lemon juice to prevent them from discoloring.

Strange Carrot Dessert

The idea for this unusual recipe stems from the Indian dessert of carrot halva.

SERVES 4 – 6
4 tbsp unsalted butter
1/3 cup slivered almonds
1 lb carrots, finely grated   rated
1/2 cup superfine sugar
3 tbsp rose water
juice of 3 oranges
whipped cream to serve

Melt the butter and stir fry the almonds until they are lightly browned. Use a slotted spoon to remove them from the pan, drain them on absorbent paper towels and set aside.

Add the carrots to the butter remaining in the pan and stir fry them for 15 minutes, or until they are a deep golden color. Stir in the sugar and rose water, and stir fry until the sugar melts. Continue cooking, adding a little orange juice every few minutes to keep the carrots moist. When all the orange juice is added, carry on stir frying the mixture until the excess moisture has evaporated and the carrot shreds are soft and juicy – 10 – 15 minutes in total.

Transfer the carrot mixture to a serving dish and top with the almonds. Allow to cool until just warm, then serve topped with whipped cream. Alternatively, the carrot mixture may be chilled and served cold.

STRANGE CARROT DESSERT

COEUR A LA CREME WITH SPICED PLUMS

Coeur à la Crème with Spiced Plums

Traditionally, *coeur à la crème* is set in small heart-shaped moulds with perforated bases. The drained cheese mixture is firm enough to turn out. Prepare the *coeur à la crème* a day ahead so that it has sufficient time to drain and set.

SERVES 4
225 g/8 oz curd cheese
4 tbsp caster sugar
150 ml/1/4 pint whipping cream,
   lightly whipped
knob of butter
450 g/1 lb firm plums, halved and
   stoned
2 tsp ground cinnamon
1/4 tsp ground cloves
1/2 tsp ground mixed spice
100 g/4 oz sugar

Beat the curd cheese and sugar together, then fold in the whipped cream. Line the base of four ramekin dishes with a circle of greaseproof paper. Divide the cheese mixture between the dishes, pressing it down flat. Cover with muslin, tying it in place securely (or use elastic bands). Invert the dishes on a wire rack and stand the rack in a dish. Chill the cheeses for 24 hours.

To serve the cheeses, remove the muslin and slide the blade of a knife around the inside of the dishes to loosen the cheeses. Invert each one in turn onto an individual serving plate. Chill until the plums are cooked.

Melt the butter and stir fry the plums for 1 minute. Add all the spices and continue stir frying for a further 2 minutes. Tip in the sugar and cook, stirring less briskly, until the juice runs from the plums and the sugar dissolves to form a spicy syrup.

Arrange the spiced plums on the plates alongside the *coeur à la crème* and serve immediately.

Yogurt Delight

SERVES 4

3 cups Greek yogurt
grated zest and juice of 1 orange
¼ – ⅓ cup clear honey
knob of unsalted butter
⅓ cup shelled pistachio nuts
½ cup Brazil nuts, roughly
   chopped

⅓ cup raisins
2 firm pears, peeled, cored and
   diced
¾ cup ready-to-eat dried apricots,
   sliced
½ cup seedless grapes, halved

Mix the yogurt, orange zest and 2 – 3 tablespoons of the honey, then divide it between four dishes and chill well.

Melt the butter, then stir fry the pistachios and Brazils with the raisins for 3 minutes. Add the pears and continue to stir fry for about 3 minutes, or until the pears are lightly cooked. Stir in the apricots and orange juice and bring to a boil. Boil, stirring, for 2 minutes to reduce the orange juice.

Stir in the grapes and remaining honey (or to taste) and heat through briefly. Spoon the fruit and nut mixture on top of the chilled yogurt and serve at once.

Ratafia Cherries

Ratafia biscuits are miniature almond macaroons, usually on sale in delicatessen shops or larger supermarkets.

SERVES 4

4 tbsp unsalted butter
1 lb cherries, pitted
1 tbsp clear honey

⅓ cup kirsch
¼ lb ratafia biscuits
whipped cream, fromage frais or
   natural yogurt to serve

Melt the butter and stir fry the cherries for 3–5 minutes until they begin to change color, but do not burst and become too soft.

Stir in the honey and kirsch and toss the fruit well to coat it in the sauce. Remove the pan from the heat, add the ratafia biscuits and mix them in briskly. Immediately spoon the fruit and biscuit mixture into four serving dishes. Top each portion with cream, fromage frais or yogurt, then serve at once.

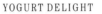

YOGURT DELIGHT

Banana and Avocado Crunch

SERVES 4

2 ripe avocados
2 bananas
juice of 1 lemon
3 tbsp confectioners sugar
⅔ cup whipping cream, whipped
4 tbsp unsalted butter

4 thick slices white bread, crusts
   removed and made into
   breadcrumbs
¾ cup walnut pieces, chopped
⅓ cup raw brown sugar
1 tsp ground cinnamon

Halve, pit and peel the avocado. Mash the avocado flesh with the bananas and lemon juice. Stir in the confectioners sugar. Reserve some of the whipped cream for decorating, spooning it into a piping bag fitted with a star nozzle. Fold the rest of the cream into the avocado mixture. Cover and chill.

Melt the butter and stir fry the breadcrumbs until they are golden brown and crisp. Stir in the walnuts, sugar and cinnamon, and continue to cook briefly. Allow to cool slightly.

Place a layer of avocado mixture in four dishes, then divide half the crumb mixture between them. Top with the remaining avocado mixture, then cover with the rest of the crumbs. Decorate with swirls of whipped cream and serve at once.

BANANA AND AVOCADO CRUNCH

MANGO AND BANANA SLICES

Mango and Banana Slices

SERVES 4

4 slices plain cake
⅓ cup sherry
4 tbsp unsalted butter
1 ripe, but firm, mango peeled,
   pitted and sliced

¼ cup redcurrant jelly
3 bananas, sliced
3 tbsp orange juice

Divide the cake slices between four plates and sprinkle a spoonful of sherry over each portion.

Melt half the butter and stir fry the mango slices for 1 – 2 minutes, until they are hot. Add the redcurrant jelly and continue stir frying for a minute or so until the jelly melts and coats the mango. Divide the mango slices between the four plates, arranging them on top of the cake. Scrape all the juices from the pan over the mango.

Melt the remaining butter and briskly stir fry the banana slices until hot. Sprinkle the orange juice over the banana, then stir for a few seconds to heat the juices. Spoon the bananas over the mango slices and serve at once.

Custards with Caramelized Fruit

Vary the fruit according to the season or your budget –
combine exotics, such as mango, pawpaw and
mangosteen with chunks of pear or pineapple; or cook
some apples until golden and add some raisins and a
swirl of rum.

SERVES 4

2½ cups of milk
2 eggs
2 egg yolks
¼ cup sugar
knob of unsalted butter
1 tbsp walnut oil

1 pineapple, peeled, cored and
  cubed
⅓ cup orange juice
⅓ cup dark soft brown sugar
4 oranges, peeled and segments
  removed

Set the oven at 325°F. Have a roasting pan ready to hold
the dishes of custard and a kettle of boiling water.
Butter four ramekin dishes. Heat the milk until almost
boiling, then remove from the heat.

Beat the eggs and yolks with the sugar, then whisk in
the milk. Strain the custards into the four dishes and
stand them in the roasting pan. Pour in boiling water to
two-thirds of the way up the sides of the ramekin dishes.
Cover with greased waxed paper and bake for 40
minutes, or until the custards are set. Leave to cool in
the pan, then chill well, preferably overnight.

Invert the custards on to four serving plates before
stir frying the pineapple. Melt the butter with the walnut
oil, then stir fry the pineapple for 3 minutes. Add the
orange juice and stir in the brown sugar. Continue to
cook, stirring, until the sugar melts and the liquid boils.
Boil for a few minutes until the syrup is reduced and
caramelized.

Remove the pan from the heat and add the orange
segments. Spoon the fruit and caramel around and over
the custards and serve at once.

Cinnamon Apples and Apricots

SERVES 4

4 eating apples, peeled, cored
  and quartered
juice of ½ lemon
⅓ cup superfine sugar

1 tbsp ground cinnamon
knob of butter
1 lb fresh apricots, halved and
  pitted

Toss the apple quarters in lemon juice. Mix the sugar
and cinnamon, then toss the moist apple quarters in it to
coat them as evenly as possible.

Melt the butter and stir fry the apples until they are
lightly caramelized outside. Add the apricots and
continue stir frying for about 3 minutes, depending on
the ripeness of the apricots, until the apricot halves are
tender and hot. Transfer to four serving dishes and
serve at once.

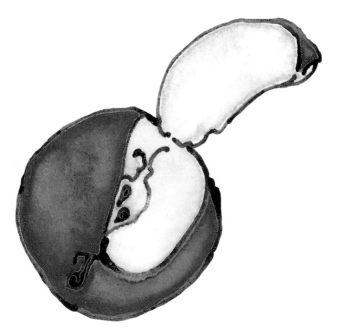

INDEX